Tempus ORAL HISTORY *Series*

Droylsden and Audenshaw
voices

Outside 'Larchwood' on Sandy Lane, Droylsden, where Jeanne Margerison (née Nixon) lived as a child, around 1930. Jeanne, on the right, with her friends Lucy and Jean Morton (left), remembers the lanes and farm land, where she played, and Moorside primary school, where she was both pupil and teacher.

Tempus ORAL HISTORY *Series*

Droylsden and Audenshaw
voices

Compiled by
Jill Cronin

TEMPUS

Tempus Publishing Limited
The Mill, Brimscombe Port,
Stroud, Gloucestershire, GL5 2QG

ISBN 0 7524 2199 9

Typesetting and origination by
Tempus Publishing Limited
Printed in Great Britain by
Midway Colour Print, Wiltshire

Acknowledgements

I should like to thank all those people, who have contributed their memories and photographs. I am grateful to Denton Local History Society for allowing me to use the small Audenshaw collection of interviews, taped mainly by Marion Pilcher over the years. Special thanks go to John Lysons, a fellow member of Denton Local History Society, who has joined me in the painstaking task of transcribing and then typing up the taped memories. Grateful thanks go also to Lena Slack for generously allowing me to use excerpts from her autobiography, and to Arthur Bantoft for his own and his mother's memories. I thank everyone for allowing me to include their memories and photographs in this book, including Norah Thorley, Audrey Butterworth and Alice Lock of Stalybridge Local Studies Library.

Contents

Introduction

When I compiled *Denton Voices* together with Marion Pilcher in 1998, we had to hand the large archive of taped memories in Denton Local History Society and also many transcripts of the tapes, already prepared by Marion. While compiling *Droylsden and Audenshaw* in 1998, I made many friends, who have vivid memories of growing up, living and working in Audenshaw and Droylsden and whom I have spent the last year revisiting and taping their memories. It has been a privilege to spend many hours, reviving images of the towns as they were, looking at photographs from family albums and always being refreshed with welcome cups of tea. One visit has led to another, to family friends or relatives.

The pile of tapes grew steadily and the hours of work I had ahead of me, listening, transcribing by hand and then typing out, were speeded up and shared by John Lysons. A minimum of editing has been carried out. There are small changes to improve readability and to shorten long extracts but the tone and speech of each individual have always been preserved as far as possible. The memory does sometimes play tricks. The names of people, the places mentioned and the dates given are as accurate only as the memories of the people who supplied them.

It suddenly struck me how many generations we have lost since Marion began her taping back in the 1980s. *Denton Voices* included memories of the Boer War and the late 1800s, but these are of people, who were either children or young married couples during the Second World War. Their recollections of parents and grandparents take us back to the early 1900s. The oldest lady I was privileged to meet was Mrs Ruth Rogerson who, born in 1898, at the age of 102 described her own early memories of Guide Lane, housework and the First World War.

The chapters range from childhood, schooldays and working life to leisure activities and the local area. While covering many aspects of both towns' history, there are gaps as not every school, church, mill, farm or shopping area could be included. I have tried to create a balance in each chapter but inevitably the material depends on whom I have visited and what areas of town life they were involved in. There is more taping to be done, before we lose forever recollections of farming, work in the cotton, mining and hatting industries, shopping along lost centres like Guide Lane, past leisure activities, and areas of the two towns that have been transformed for ever. It is encouraging that while this book has been in preparation, Kenneth Whittaker has produced an outline history of Audenshaw called *Saltway to Motorway* and both Audenshaw Local History Society and also Tameside Local History Forum have been formed. I hope that this collection of tapes will be the beginning of an oral history archive for Audenshaw. It would be good to have also a home in Droylsden for the Droylsden tapes.

I have really enjoyed making and using these tape recordings. Memories of childhoods spent in difficult and often hard circumstances during the wars, and the Depression of the late 1920s and 1930s are vivid and touching, but also full of humour and resilience. I hope that all those resident now in Droylsden and Audenshaw will enjoy hearing from other people's lips what life was like in the last century. There are many former residents living abroad or elsewhere in Britain, some of whom have their memories in this book. For them this should prove a nostalgic but realistic read about their hometown. For newcomers and for younger readers, I hope that this book will help them discover that both towns have fascinating and interesting, but steadily changing areas, and that the older residents experienced much in their early lives that should be passed on to future generations. If this book inspires someone to go and tape their grandparents, great grandparents or elderly neighbours, to join or form a local history society, or to carry out their own research into their area or family history, then it has all been worthwhile.

Jill Cronin
February 2001

The workers of S.D. Ainsworth & Son in the early 1900s outside the Richmond Works in Audenshaw, where they produced hat bodies as part of the process of hat making. Mavis Langridge's grandfather, Samuel Ainsworth, founded the business, which then passed down to her father, Reginald, who is kneeling first right in the front row, next to his brother Harold.

A school photograph at St Andrew's, Droylsden, in 1947, belonging to Joyce Wild (née Goodwin), who now lives in Devon. Before Droylsden High School was opened, this school provided three classes for girls over the age of eleven, with Miss Lee as head teacher and Miss Nightingale and Mrs Howarth as teachers.

Dorothy Lord (née Vardy) stands centre in the back row in a photograph at Fairfield Road Primary School, Droylsden, in the late 1930s. Her memories of growing up in the 1930s and 1940s convey realistically and vividly the harsh times of the Depression and the Second World War.

CHAPTER 1
Childhood

Members of St Hilda's Sunday school in a concert in 1923 outside the Sunday school, where Audenshaw Community Centre now stands. Fourth from the right at the front is Bessie Watt (née Clark) and at the back, wearing a helmet, stands Carrie, the maid at the vicarage, who came from Trafalgar House Orphanage.

Playing Out

We used to play outside a lot. At the back of the house there was 'the big backs'. We called them 'backs', and no-one could get in, only us. We used to play 'school' and go in one another's gardens and have little concerts. We used to play 'Hide and Seek', until Vera's father came and chased us off.

He said, 'Go and play in your own back!'

Rose Perfect

Kick Can

We used to have seasons for the games. Boys used to play a game with marbles and cigarette cards. The boys would play football but they couldn't afford a football, because balls were rather dear – a whole sixpence. They kicked to one another an empty, squashed can. This was called 'Kick Can'. What a noise it made on the cobblestones! We girls had wooden dollies which we made clothes for and we used to play hop-scotch. We also had whips and tops; we used to colour the tops so that, when we got them spinning, they made lovely patterns. We also had balls and skipping ropes made out of plaited straw, which we used to get from the greengrocer's. You see, this rope was tied round crates of oranges. It made excellent skipping ropes but unfortunately, if you couldn't skip very well, it used to lash the back of your legs and make them hurt.

Vera Worth

John Pearson, aged three in 1932, stands outside his grandparents' home. His mother ran a corner shop on Moorside Street, Droylsden.

Benny Lane

We used to go down Benny Lane as children. There was a stile just past World's End Farm and you were in an open field with a ditch by the path. I can remember one of our favourite activities was, if we found a dead bird or anything else, we'd have a service and make a grave and bury them under the tree. There was a particular hawthorn bush there. There were hawthorn bushes all the way down Benny Lane and all the way past the houses up the Moss, as far as the second gate. That was the limit of where you were allowed out to play. We used to walk down Benny Lane through that field where we used to bury the dead birds, to the level crossing, then walk across the railway line and a little path through there that brings you back to Jaum Farm. We used to pick wild flowers. I had a book that I used to press flowers in and write about them.

Jeanne Margerison

Playing Football

I remember Dale's Pig Farm which was at the end of Benny Lane. Beyond there were some very, very rough fields in which we used to play football. It must have been a very peculiar game when I think about it, because it was not flat at all; it was full of tufts of grass and things. In the summertime I know people set it on fire and you used to beat it out with your coat. It never seemed to do any damage because there wasn't anything to damage as far as I could see.

John Pearson

Hanging on the Back

As children we all played games in the street, as there was hardly any traffic. The Rag and Bone man came round and Granelli's ice cream cart with a horse pulling it. We used to hang on the back on our roller skates and were always getting told off. We spent a lot of time on Lewis Road playing fields before the park was there. There was a big house near the corner of Manor and Lewis Roads. It had a lovely garden. It was empty: I used to think it was haunted. All the children used to go in but I wouldn't.

Joyce Wild

Belling Up

One game we played invoked some memory of Audenshaw's rural past and involved two or three of us 'belling up' – that is interlocking arms at the back like horses harnessed together and being driven along by a boy behind. There was quite a bit of house building in the area. Ash Street was already built up on the opposite side from the school but the rest of the land between Sidmouth Street and the railway was built on during these years. The partly built houses were ideal places to play in, and when we were tired of that we could cross the railway line to play on the 'prairie' on the other side. The stream provided much amusement and we refreshed ourselves from a stone-lined drain which emerged from under some cinder in-fill. How we did not suffer broken limbs from falling on the building site, or death on the railway or from some foul water-borne diseases, I shall never know. There were many more childhood deaths than there are now. I can remember

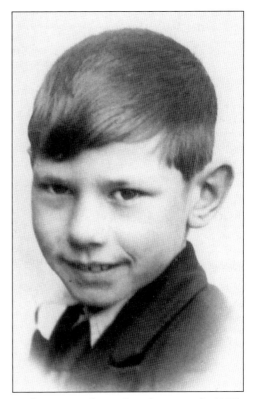

Arthur Bantoft aged eight around 1937. Arthur's recording of his mother, Annie Beesley's memories brings to life the area around Red Hall, Audenshaw, in the early 1900s. Arthur also relives his childhood and his schooldays at Audenshaw Grammar School in the 1930s and 1940s.

two schoolgirls dying during my time at Lumb Lane and Eric says that two boys died of typhoid from drinking the water in the farm pond.

The wooden bridge spanning the railway at the back was a great focus for our activities, as was the brickyard, although this was still working. It came into its own later on during the war years when work was suspended and it began to take on the form of a wilderness.

Arthur Bantoft

Harry Slater aged six in 1933 on holiday with his mother, Mary Elizabeth (Lizzie) (née Taylor).

Playing Peggy

In the 1930s, between the house and the railway station [Hooley Hill], which has now got houses on, there was a great big plot of land. All the lads in the area used to come and play on. There was room for a football pitch. During certain times of the year, lads used to come on there playing 'peggy'. A little piece of wood is the peggy, about three inches long and about one inch in diameter and tapered off at one side. You had a stick and the peggy used to be on a brick and, as you hit the tapered part of the peggy, it used to jump up in the air and with the stick you then hit it as far as you could. One team

used to say, 'Right, that's twenty strides: you can have that for eighteen, if you can do it'. The other team used to try and get a jumper then to jump it in eighteen strides and, if they jumped it, they scored eighteen. If they didn't jump it in eighteen strides, the team that had knocked it scored twenty. It got a bit out of hand and they used to start having bets on the games. Eventually they were stopped from gambling. They used to play glass marbles on there and you used to win marbles off other people. The one with the largest bag was the best marble player.

Harry Slater

School Milk

School milk was supplied daily in the 1930s, small bottles with a cardboard top with an inner circle, which could be pierced with a straw. The cardboard tops we kept: two tops were placed together and wool was wound through the inner circle, until it was filled. The outer area was then cut around the full circle, the two tops gently eased apart and a length of wool tied between the two circles to make the wool secure. The cardboard circles were eased off and the fluffy ball we made was shaken and used to decorate wool hats, or a bunch of wool balls were hung on a crotcheted length of wool, making a chain and hung in baby's pram, as something for baby to look at and enjoy the movement as they swung to and fro.

At primary school, we had a savings bank. I was encouraged to save by my grandfather, who gave me a 3d piece weekly. This was for saving, *not* for spending. My grandmother bought me *Girls Crystal Weekly*, which I read avidly.

Dorothy Lord

Flying Circus

I can remember the 1935 General Election when we went round chalking 'Vote for Gibson' (the Labour Candidate), until someone suggested that we ought to write 'Vote for Hopkinson' instead, which we then did. About that time, a flying circus came to Reddish. I suppose we had permission to go and there would be older children in charge, but we walked the length of King's Road to see the display from outside the ground. It was a long walk back.

Arthur Bantoft

Sweets in the Family

My first memories are going to visit my grandma; she'd taken over the shop in 1913 and it was on the corner of Stamford Road, opposite the Pack Horse there. We used to love going there: it was children's paradise with all those sweets! As we grew older, she let us help in the shop, which we liked. When she passed away, my aunt took over and I used to help all the years then. We were allowed to go Saturday afternoon and serve the children for the matinée that was across the road at the Stamford cinema. We used to love doing that, serving out of the little jars on the counter. I had to stand on a buffet: I was only about eight. We got 6d for that and saved it up for our holiday. They built that little asbestos hut and I used to go there [St Hilda's]. Inside there were chairs everywhere, not pews; it was modern. The vicar was called Mr Clarke. I liked going with Granny Green, because she always used to have mint imperials and when the sermon was on, we had them to keep us quiet.

Joan Jebb

Naughty Boy!

My mother had a milliner's shop on Guide Lane and we were there until about 1915; I was either four or five. If my mother went grey early, it was because of me! On one occasion she heard a lot of laughter and wondering what was going on, went to have a look and I was actually in the window trying hats on and a crowd had collected outside. On another occasion, when she heard a lot of noise and went in, I had one or two of my pals there and was emptying the till and handing the money out!

Austin Hopkinson's election picture, when he stood as candidate for the Mossley Parliamentary division in 1945. He owned the Delta Works at Audenshaw, and lived at Ryecroft Hall, which he generously gave to the town to use as council offices.

Fred Clark in July 1929, standing first on the right with his family, in the fields behind his home on Denton Road, Audenshaw, with Kilshaw Lane in the background. The family includes his father Walter, mother Alice, his elder brother Edgar, his sister Mary and his youngest sister, Bessie Watt, who also contributes memories of her childhood.

It wasn't that I didn't like home but I used to wander: I used to disappear and they would have to send out the coal man and the bread man and the milkman: 'Had they seen me?' You only had to walk to the end of the street and along a dirt track and you came to this railway bridge. On the Sheffield side of Guide Bridge station there was this iron bridge that went across, and I suppose in a way, for a tot it was dangerous, because if you went down these steps at the other side, there was the Ashton Canal which ran past it. I used to spend hours on that bridge. It was fascinating: they had the huge sidings and the trains used to shunt and, when they shunted, the locomotives often came under the bridge with the steam. You were covered in steam and everything was black.

St Anne's Road went through to St Anne's church in Denton. There were Quakers that lived in this house; they had a grocery shop almost opposite the end of Shepley Road on Guide Lane. They were two brothers who were Quakers, and they wore stove pipe hats. We used to hide behind a wall when they went past and we used to shout 'Beaver!' and then run. I think I was twelve, so it would have been 1922.

Fred Clark

Hooley Hill Station in the 1930s

When we used to come on our holidays from London back to Manchester because the family was here, we used to stay at my aunt's, who lived on Guide Lane, just up from the smithy. Her two sons, myself and my cousin Ivy, we would go out exploring and we could get out onto the station from the playing fields, down below Mount Pleasant Street. There was a tunnel that led from the station and came out on the farm land by Saxon Farm. They took us through this railway tunnel. It was still being used: the line was still open. When we got back home, we were sworn to secrecy. My youngest cousin Geoffrey, aged about three, was having his bath in front of the fire. My aunt said, 'What have you been doing today?' He said, 'Oh! We've been through the railway tunnel!'

Bill Pollitt

Hooley Hill

We were right by the side. There was a lot of train movement. They used to come from Stockport area through from Denton station, through past the brickyard in Audenshaw, along Guide Lane and through to Guide Bridge and on there, then some off to Leeds. It was during the Beeching thing that it closed. It was quite an active little station: they'd quite a few guards on duty and ticket people. The entrance was on Mount Pleasant Street with wooden staircases down to the platforms. The kids used to come and play on there. They used to get chased by the porters. It was dangerous on the line but we used to play running up and down the staircase.

Harry Slater

Our Brickyard Playground

Where it's all now nice, flat, level ground from the back of the council houses on Guide Lane through to Stamford Road, that was the brickyard area. They had dug and dug clay out until there were three main holes, quite deep, and we used to use these as mountains and play Cowboys and Indians. Then they used to fill with water. Fish came in these ponds and we used to fish for them with a cane and a piece of string and a bent pin. We used to catch gudgeon and sometimes small sticklebacks. We were always told as boys as we hadn't got to swim in the brickyard, as the water was dirty. So our parents wouldn't know we'd been in, we just stripped everything off. We didn't have any bathing costumes, as they'd have known where we were going. We swam in the dirty, brown water, came out and just dried off by running round. It was good in the winter, because the ponds used to freeze over quite thick. It was safe to skate on. I had a pair of ice skates eventually and we used to go and skate on there.

Harry Slater

Skating

We used to go skating on the ponds of the brickyard. They weren't deep ponds. My friends had clogs. A lot of people still wore clogs after the war. The beauty of them was, if you went on the snow and ice, it built up between the irons of the clogs and you could skate quite well on the brickyard. I had only shoes.

Bill Pollitt

Music and Reading

When I was nearly four, in 1924, I had a toy piano. It was a beauty, with a dark, polished wooden case, and I remember that it had '12s 6d' marked on the underside of the lid. It had about twenty-four notes, and soon I could play the songs we had learned at school for Christmas, *A Star was Shining in the Sky*, with all the twiddly bits that Miss Saxon, our teacher, used to add in the accompaniment. I found I had only to hear a tune a time or two and then I could play it. So, a year or two later, having seen a real little mini piano in

Lena Slack (née Johnson) with her elder sister Betty in the garden of the Blue Pig public house on Audenshaw Road, in the early 1920s, where her mother worked at one time. Lena's autobiography gives a detailed account of growing up near Red Hall chapel in the aftermath of the First World War and the hard times of the Depression.

Northend's shop in Denton, my mother made up her mind to buy it for me for Christmas. It cost £3 10s 0d and she secured it with a 10s deposit. Later she paid another 10s but my father went on short time at the mill; so she had to ask for her pound back and I didn't get my piano.

I learned to read by taking a book 'from the shop', to bed and returning it to stock next morning. I could only have been about three years old when I began to pick out letters first of all from the tin of condensed milk on the kitchen table. It was 'COW' brand, with a picture of a cow, and over the animal, the word 'COW' in large ornate letters arranged in an arc. Then I recall asking my mother what 'elect' meant on the tin of 'Rowntree's Elect Cocoa', and one of my earliest recollections is of the sign, 'Ales and Stout' over a public house. I asked whether it was pronounced 'All-es', and my mother described ale as beer, and ales meant different kinds of beer.

How I longed for us to have a hall and a hallstand: Christopher Robin had a nanny and had a dressing gown hung on the door. I saw pictures of children in the bathroom, whilst I washed at the slop stone and bathed on the hearth. Similarly, our books had pictures of houses with gardens and a swing, whilst we had a backyard. But the hall, the bathroom and the garden were ambitions to achieve by hard work. Books where the children had a nanny, a cook and a gardener lifted me out of my dull surroundings on to another plane.

Lena Slack

Cycling

When I was about nine or ten in 1920, Uncle Jim gave me a bicycle. It had cane ribs and no brakes: they were never straight.

It depended on the weather; they used to warp. Good job my father and mother didn't know what I got up to! I remember the only way you could stop was to put your foot on the wheel. Well sometimes, if you were going very fast, the wheel would drag your foot and so you got it stuck in the forks. Then of course you wouldn't come to a full stop, you couldn't get your foot out and so you would fall on the floor with the bike. I remember alongside Denton station, between the reservoir and the railway line, there were railway sleepers all along, there was dirt and, as it came out onto Manchester Road, it went up a slope. You could belt like mad down there and then the slope would slow you down enough to come out. I remember going along there one day; I was going like the clappers. I was terrified actually because there was a tramcar just near the top of the hill and I just shot in front of it, the driver banging his bell like mad. I was terrified because I shouldn't have been doing that anyway. I belted like the clappers all the way down to Debdale and then dashed into Debdale Park out of the way, hoping nobody had seen me. Often, when I got a proper bike and went out, mother would say, 'Fred, be careful!' I used to say 'Mother, I'm always careful: it's these other idiots. It's not me!'

Fred Clark

Fred Clark stands by the pond on Clayton's farm land behind his house on Denton Road, Audenshaw, in July 1929. Fred recounts his antics as a youngster and teenager, as he explored the surrounding countryside of his youth.

Sharing a Bike

I dearly wanted a bicycle. My grandfather was an enterprising man. He bought a bicycle without a crossbar, which he let me borrow. He made a bar of metal round it, which clipped on to form a man's bike with a cross bar for his use and so we shared the one bicycle. There was little chance of having one of my own. The bicycle was heavy but what enjoyment!

Dorothy Lord

Taking Dad's Dinner to the Mill

In the 1920s, as the buzzer sounded at twelve noon, I shot out of school to be met by my mother, holding a basin tied up in a red handkerchief, and giving off a steaming odour of cabbage, peas or potato pie. Then a rush for the tram where that particular smell became mingled with those from the other dishes on the day's menu. As the tram grated its way along the mile to the mill, we sat, if we were lucky, or strap-hung, with an ever watchful eye on the red bundle to keep it steady, lest we spill the gravy. We didn't have baskets, but gripped the tight knot, on top of the saucer which covered the basin, with tense fingers, which would be quite numb by the time they relinquished their bundle.

The mill stopped at a quarter past twelve and so sometimes, if the tram was early, the mules would still be running as I toiled up and up four flights of stone steps to the top-floor, where dad worked as a minder in the spinning room. At the door of the room, I was met by the warm, humid air and the smell of raw cotton and oil. Walking gingerly on the slippery floor, I would sidle along the narrow alley between the wall and the first pair of mules. As I walked, the little wheels would creep up, nearer and nearer, and then turn and run away again and then again came towards me. I never got over the feeling that one day they would run on and on and over my toes. At the end of the alley, my father would be working in a Union shirt, blue bib and brace overalls and bare feet. I couldn't hear his greeting, as the noise of the machinery drowned all other sounds but I'd wave to him, and suddenly, quite suddenly, the wheels would stop, the overhead straps quiver and all would be still. Dad would come towards me with his white enamelled brew can, sit down on the floor and eat his dinner, still piping hot, from the white basin.

Lena Slack

Getting Our Own Back!

We were living on Maddison Avenue. My father [the local lamp lighter] chastised us one day and we were all sent to bed and we were very annoyed. We were going to get our own back on him. We were having company coming round, we were going to miss it all, and we'd been sent to bed at around seven o'clock instead of nine. Fortunately we had a catapult upstairs with a few pebbles and, just outside the house, there was a lamp. We aimed repeatedly at this lamp to crack it. Every so often we would hit it with a stone and then dive into bed but we didn't manage to break it until the very last stone, when we cracked it and triumphantly went to bed. But it really did rebound on us because, as the lamp was outside our own home, it was one that none of his bosses was likely to see, as it wasn't on the main road, and it was left for weeks before it was repaired. We looked at this and thought, 'Dad has to repair that and we've done that' and so we were quite sorry by the end.

David Langridge

Feeling Ill

When we were ill or poorly, as we used to say, our mums and grans always had their own remedy for coughs and colds. But if you were really ill, mum used to take us to the doctor's surgery where we would be examined, given a bottle of medicine and charged 2s 6d. Sometimes, if you were seriously ill, mum called the doctor to visit the house; then the charge was 3s 6d. This was a lot of money in those days and the doctor would hire a man to call at your house every week until the debt was paid. He was known as the doctor's man and we paid him 3d each week.

Vera Worth

Scarlet Fever

I did get scarlet fever: I had to be isolated, which was difficult and for the short time I was at home, a damp blanket was hung at the bedroom door, hopefully to deter the fever from spreading. I went into an isolation ward at Monsall Hospital. The only way my family could visit was by climbing the fire escape staircase at the hospital and waving to me at the window. I am sure this was against any hospital rules but it was a comfort to wave back, after what must have been a long journey for them plus a climb up the staircase!

Dorothy Lord

Home Remedies

Because it was expensive to call the doctor, homely remedies were widely known and used. As soon as the clocks were altered in October, a square of camphor sewn into a little cotton bag would be hung around my neck to guard against colds. Sitting at my school desk, I would hunch my shoulders, wriggle my chin inside the neck of my woolly jumper, and draw up a warm, comforting wave of camphorated air into my nasal cavities.

For a sore throat, we gargled with vinegar and warm water, or 'flowers of sulphur' were blown through a paper tube into the back of one's throat. A hot potato

in a woollen stocking was a remedy for quinsy. Rashers of fatty bacon were worn round the throat, or goose grease, spread on flannel, was applied to the chest. This latter had a most sickly, nauseous smell. I remember taking a stone jar to our nearby farm and having it filled with goose grease at a cost of 4d. The inside of a raw swede, scraped out and mixed with brown sugar, was a not unpleasant cough cure for a child.

If you were really ill and the doctor came and ordered you to stay in bed, there was

The top class from Poplar Street day school, Audenshaw, on a trip to Chester Cathedral in the 1920s. Seated centre is the head teacher, Mr Armitage, and standing second on the left in the middle in a white hat is Vera Worth (née Chapman).

the fire in the bedroom grate, and the luxury of falling asleep with the firelight flickering on the walls. On cold winter nights my mother would wrap the 'oven shelf' in a 1d piece of blanket, and it would retain its heat for hours. If a doctor's bill was incurred, it came with the doctor's name and a handsome copper-plated heading, with many curls and scrolls, and including his 'letters' (as we called his qualifications). The amount owing would be collected in coppers by the doctor's man, (James H. Pinkerton), who called every Tuesday dinner time. He took a fountain pen, (the first I ever saw) from his vest pocket and, unscrewing the cap, deducted usually 6d in old money, signing his initials on the bill itself, so that it looked like one big sum extending down the paper. It was likely that whilst that bill was being paid off, another would have been presented, for attendance on some other member of the family.

I remember the grandchild of our neighbour being taken to the Isolation Hospital with diphtheria on a winter afternoon when the light was going. We stood in awe-stricken silence as the little girl was carried out on a stretcher (another fearsome object) and put into the ambulance. As the vehicle bumped its way out of our pot-holed, unmade street, my mother whispered, 'Poor little lamb', and wiped away a tear.

Lena Slack

On Holiday

We used to walk a lot in the 1920s, because people didn't have cars, so we didn't go far away from Audenshaw. Sometimes we visited Ashton Market. The fare was 1s 2d for a child. We saw one or two aeroplanes which used to write smoke messages in the sky like 'Compo' which was the washing powder everyone used. I used to love this; it was fun seeing the words being blown away by the wind. Of course, if you were lucky, you and your parents could afford a week's holiday. You went on a great adventure by train. Blackpool was the main resort and how we loved it, dad carrying the luggage and mum looking after the family.

Vera Worth

Staying on a Farm

In the 1930s grandfather and father worked for the railway company. This entitled them to free passes to travel by rail. Our world opened up, as we travelled to Anglesey and stayed at a working farm. This we did for a few years. Hot water at the farm had to be carried upstairs by the farmer's wife to the guests – our family. Food was prepared by the farmer's wife – eggs, milk, honey, buttermilk, fresh from the farm. There were cows and sheep, hens and turkeys – so different a life. I made a friend of the farmer's daughter. She came over at times to stay at my grandparents'. My family had no room with our family of six and I stayed with her at my grandparents' home – happy times! The toilet at the farm was in a small orchard near the farmhouse and it had a wooden, square seat, central hole, and a tin container inside, which had to be emptied by the farmer.

Dorothy Lord

Ryecroft Hall

My grandparents were caretakers in the 1960s; I just loved the place. When we were little, we used to have birthday parties in the downstairs ballroom. If we were very, very good, we were allowed to play in the upstairs ballroom, where there was a lovely polished floor. We used to take our shoes off and skate all along it.

My auntie, my mum's sister, had two boys that were more or less the same age as my brother and I and they lived in Droylsden. So they spent as much time there as I and my brother. We'd play hide and seek down the corridors. I think it's still like that in the back part of the hall, at the back of the house. There was a seat, then a piece of wood and then another seat, all part of the panelling. So dad used to hide and we'd come running out. It would be pitch black and dad'd jump out from behind the panels and frighten the life out of us. It was a great place for hide and seek. We knew our way around the attics and the boilers, because I used to help my grandpa stoke the boiler, which I suppose was very, very dangerous but in those days I don't think people worried so much, did they?

One thing I do remember was the dumb waiter in the back kitchen. We tried to get my youngest cousin, Glyn, to go in but, fortunately, auntie came along and rescued him. I don't think it would have taken his weight. You went out into a little square hall and the front door was there, and then to the right there was the best lounge, where we weren't really allowed to play but I used to get in, because the piano was there and this huge bay window with a window seat. I used to pretend I was a princess and sit on this window seat.

Dorothy Lord (née Vardy) aged about eight in 1936. Dorothy was brought up in Droylsden, being the town's Carnival Queen in 1949.

We had lots of games in the grounds, because I remember it before the library was built in the grounds. There were two groundsmen: Little Arthur, he was actually a midget, so everybody called him Little Arthur and a very, very tall man, called Ernest. They used to chase the children away but we were allowed in and we were allowed to climb the trees. But I don't really think he dared to say 'No' to grandma, because she was quite formidable, when she wanted to be. It was open as a park then but they didn't like children wandering around. Of course, the bowling green was there and the house was open, because it was the council offices. In front of the bowling green there was the putting green. So you used to

Kate Kerry (née Newton) in the arms of her grandfather, Bill Bradshaw, in the front sitting room at Ryecroft Hall, Audenshaw around 1956. William and Sarah Bradshaw were the caretakers at the hall, where Kate spent many happy hours.

have to go and ask Arthur; I think it was 2d. I think we used to play on it more than anyone else.

Kate Kerry

Living at the YMCA

I was born in the YMCA at No. 36, Denton Road, Audenshaw. My parents were the caretakers there in the late 1920s and we used to have two bedrooms upstairs. It must have been rather crowded because there were six boys. My parents had the front bedroom and the six boys were in the back bedroom. The three older ones had one bed in one corner, and in the diagonal corner were the three smaller boys.

We younger boys weren't allowed to go into the YMCA, unless we went with my father, which I always did on a Sunday morning, when he did quite a lot of work. We three younger boys had to sit on the forms that were all round the billiard room, which were covered in sort of leatherette cloth, which was quite prickly and I think it was full of horse hair. We had to sit there and not make a noise, while my father cleaned all the floor, ironed all the billiard tables with a flat iron, which was a rectangular iron, and generally cleaned up. We would end up with our hands under our thighs to help protect from this coarse cloth underneath us. Of course, my mother and father were always very busy and we dare not misbehave ourselves; we just sat there like good lads, unless my father went out. In which case we jumped down and ran about. I must have been very small because I could run underneath the tables and swing round on the huge legs at the corner of the billiard table.

David Langridge

Trafalgar House Orphanage

In the early1900s, on Audenshaw Road, just past the Blue Pig, was the Church of England Children's Society's home. I remember these children used to come in and they used to sit on the left-hand side at St Stephen's. These children, there must have been at least twenty of them, all dressed alike, boys and girls. They wore a sort of uniform. I mean they were quite smart; they weren't shabby or anything. I wondered what it was all about because they were all in procession with probably two grown-ups. I remember asking my mother once what they were and she said that they were for orphan boys and girls and if I didn't behave myself and cause her less trouble she'd die and I'd end up there. It terrified me to think I would have to go and dress like them.

Fred Clark

Carrie

Carrie was the maid at the vicarage. She'd come from that children's home on Audenshaw Road at the Trough. We used to invite them to all the things at St Hilda's, all the children from there.

Bessie Watt

Growing Up

We went to St Stephen's in the 1920s. There were all these boys in the choir and after church, on Sunday night, there were about ten of us used to go, boys and girls, walk along Audenshaw Road, up Groby Road to Ryecroft Park. There used to be a band there and there was this beautiful lawn and trees all round. It was a 'monkey run': all the boys used to stand under the trees and all the girls used to go round and round. Lots of people met their Waterloo there; they'd live happily ever after. We didn't parade

Fred Lord aged about eight in 1938 on his holidays at Blackpool. Fred was brought up during the Second World War in Droylsden, where his grandfather, Charles Frederick Moore, ran a haulage business.

23

David Langridge on the right, aged twelve around 1938. He is standing with his brothers, from left to right, Ronnie, Eric and Ernest, behind their house on Maddison Avenue, looking towards the canal near Lumb Lane.

round so much because we'd gone with all our boys. Eric used to buy me a quarter of Cadbury's milk tray every Sunday night, 6d they were. By the time we all had one each, that was it.

Bessie Watt

Dances

I went to St Andrew's church. There was a youth club there and some very good dances on a Saturday night. We danced to records but there was always a good attendance. As I got older, I started going to dances at the Toll Bar dance hall above the Co-op. They were great dances with live bands.

Joyce Wild

A class at Manchester Road Primary School, Droylsden, in 1946. Miss Burt is the teacher and first right at the back is Joyce Wild (née Goodwin).

The British School

The school my mother, Annie Beesley, attended, in the early 1900s, is now offices next to the Blue Pig. The school was a two-storey building. On the ground floor were two rooms, one for cookery and the other housing the infants. This had a large sloping gallery on which the children sat. Upstairs all the children were taught in the same room. Standards I to IV had individual teachers but Standards V to VII were taught together by the headmaster, Mr Knott. When he lost his temper, sparks began to fly. His pupils had scrawled his name over much of the chimney breast. He said that he didn't object to his nickname 'Paddy', as long as they gave it a capital 'P'. Writing lessons involved the

A cricket class at the British School on Audenshaw Road in the early 1900s. The head teacher at the back is Mr W.F. Knott and on the right is Pompey the dog.

laborious drawing of 'pot hooks', with 'thin strokes up and thick strokes down'. In the final year girls went downstairs to learn cookery using a gas stove. Each week a sergeant came from the barracks at Ashton to drill the boys on the open space between the school and the Blue Pig. The seniors paid between 1d and 4d as their weekly 'school pence'. Mother spent her final year as a 'half-timer', working in the morning, doing housework and errands for a local lady, and going to school in the afternoon.

Arthur Bantoft

Starting School

I went to Guide Lane to the day school as a child aged four in the 1930s. We lived at Shepley Road and my first day we had to walk to the school at the top of Garden Street. I didn't want to go to school but my mother wanted me to go. So I was actually dragged screaming up the street.

Bill Pollitt

A Special Teacher

My schooldays were spent at Littlemoss School on Lumb Lane, which in the 1930s was a church day school belonging to Christ Church, Ashton. Today it's no longer a school but has been converted into a private property. Mrs Bew used to be an exceptionally good teacher with newcomers. She paid a lot of attention to individuals. I had to go to a Manchester hospital to have my tonsils removed. Mrs Bew used to visit me and bring books with her for me to read. Then at the time of my leaving Littlemoss to come to King's Road, she bought me a parting present of a book, something that I've always treasured over many, many years.

George Walker

Mr Donnelly

In the 1960s I went to Audenshaw County primary school, which was more commonly known as Lumb Lane. We had a very eccentric teacher called Mr Donnelly: we adored him. He was the one who started me in Art. His two main interests were Art and Games, which were my favourites as well. So we'd be having a Maths lesson and he'd say, 'Let's stop. We'll do some painting.' He told us all about the Impressionists and we did all sorts of *avant-garde* things like flick painting, which you could imagine with ten year olds was very, very messy.

Mr Donnelly, pretended that he was into corporal punishment. He had two 3ft rulers. One was called Timothy and one was called George. He used to threaten that if we didn't behave he would give us a whack and once he did with Alan Betts. He bent over, gave him a whack and the ruler broke in half. Complete uproar in the class!

A class at Littlemoss Church of England day school around 1940. The teacher is Mrs Bew and George Walker, who lived and worked on farms in Littlemoss and Audenshaw, is in the back row second from the left.

A class at Audenshaw County Primary School on Lumb Lane, Audenshaw in 1960. Lena Slack was their teacher and on the first row from the front, seated third from left, is Kate Kerry (née Newton).

The head, Mr Kinder, was a lovely man, very, very strict. Everyone was frightened to death of him and you always did as he said, except my brother, Phil, who was never frightened of him. One morning in assembly Phil, who would be about six at the time, wasn't feeling very well and Mr Kinder was reading the lesson. Phil just toddled out to him and put his arms around him. Mr Kinder did the whole assembly cuddling him.

Kate Kerry

Helping Teacher

We had two teachers called the Misses Houseleys: Miss Amy was tall and straight and Miss Ethel was crippled with arthritis.

They lived in Garden Street in Audenshaw. So Mary used to walk round every morning, pick Miss Ethel's case up and carry it round to school for her, because it was a heavy, leather one. So she could carry her handbag and her walking stick. Mary got 1d a trip: so this was 9d a week, because one morning we had to go to Red Hall for cookery. So when Mary left school, she asked me if I would do it. So I did that for two years. It was when we used to get a Saturday 1d in the 1920s. It was very nice having 9d a week in one fell swoop: it was riches.

Bessie Watt

Milk for the Teachers

I went to school in 1924, my third birthday.

When I was in the infants, because I lived so near, I was usually sent to buy pies or custards at Miss Brook's corner shop for the teachers' lunches. Every morning, before I went to school, I went to the farm with a jug to collect a gill of milk for the teachers' mid-morning tea.

Lena Slack

Guide Lane Methodists'

In the 1920s, we hadn't a proper playground. The elder ones played at the front: it used to be a little market ground, right in front of the Wesleyan church on Garden Street going off Guide Lane. One friend, Dora, lived on Bank Street: so mornings we'd nip down their back and have a drink of tea at their house. Nobody knew where we'd gone and then we'd nip back, before we went in. I left when I was fourteen.

Rose Perfect

Best Fighter

I remember quite clearly every class had what they called 'the cock of the class', the one who was the best fighter. The beginning of the war, they started building some shelters on that ground at the side of the White Hart pub. When the shelters were finished, quite often, coming from school [Moorside primary], they used to meet in between the shelters there for a sort of knock-out competition to see who was 'the cock of the school' or 'cock of the class'.

Fred Lord

Keep Fit

We had sacks filled with newspapers to use as mattresses on the floor, because we hadn't got the rubber mattresses in those days. These used to be stored on the top of some cupboards. You used to have to climb up on the top of this cupboard and throw these home-made mattresses down. The biggest treat of the lot was jumping off the top of the cupboard onto these mattresses, doing belly flops.

Harry Slater

Bessie Watt (née Clark) in Brownie uniform (left), stands with her sister Mary in Guide uniform, by the pond on Clayton's farm land behind their house on Denton Road, Audenshaw, in July 1929.

The second class in the juniors at Audenshaw County Primary School on Lumb Lane, c. 1927. The head teacher is Mr Ben Greaves and the teacher Miss Annie Wamsley. On the second row from the back, third from the left, is Lena Slack (née Johnson).

Lost Lunches!

At Moorside School in the reception class, that seemed a very big room to me, there were some children who got to have a lie down in the afternoon on little camp beds but I was too old for that. You just had to put your head on a cushion on a table. We all had a pocket on the wall to put your morning lunch in: mine had an elephant on it. But it wasn't always there when you went to look for it!

Jeanne Margerison

What's Your Name?

I didn't realise for years that the school I went to then, Poplar Street Council, had only just been built. I was born in 1910 and the school was built in 1914. I did play truant, I think, once or twice. If anybody was in trouble it was always me: it was never anybody else. When I went to work for the Co-op, I remember this chap came in and said to me, 'What's your name?' I said 'Fred Clark.' 'Ah, Fred Clark, I think I know you.' I said, 'I doubt it.' He said, 'Where do you live?' I said, 'Audenshaw.' 'Oh', he said, 'whereabouts?' I said, 'I live on Denton Road.' 'No, that's not it.' I said, 'Well, we used to live in Nelson Street.' He says, 'That's it, 42, Nelson Street. I thought I knew you.' I said, 'Why?' He said, 'I was a school attendance officer: I've been to your house once or twice!'

Fred Clark

Speaking Up

One of the older teachers, oh, she had a short temper and she used to make a fist and thump you with it. I said to her, 'Please, miss, do you know you could kill people hitting like that?' So she talked to my mother, who said, 'You must chastise her if she needs it.' She said, 'Mrs Clark, I wouldn't touch your Bessie with a barge pole.' So after that she never touched me: she never touched my sister, Mary. She never touched Marion Richardson and never touched Bessie Richardson. I was seven: I was quite cheeky. I was the youngest of four. You have to stand up for yourself, don't you? They gave me a certificate dated 5.8.1932 to say I'd finished school. I've still three of my school reports – too talkative they say!

Bessie Watt

Doff Your Cap!

Mr Armitage was the headmaster [at Poplar Street]. He was wonderful, the kindest man you could ever wish. It was the boast that he never had to beat one of the children. There were some little monkeys. The boys used to come with their trousers hanging down with the backside torn out at the back. They were terribly poor. They'd have shoes only held on with a lace flopping about but they always got to wear a cap going to school. Whenever they saw a teacher in the street, they had to raise the cap. One time one didn't raise it and I remember the teacher said, 'Come out to the front. Here's the grand boy that can't be bothered to raise his hat to the teacher.' The punishment was that he was shown up in front of all the class.

Vera Worth

Fog!

I went to Poplar Street School in 1935. I used to walk across from the farm on the edge of the brick works across and up Poplar Street. I came home at lunch time. We had a lot of fog. When there was a 'peasouper', as we used to call it, they would organize parties for going home and then send a few people off together.

Betty Slater

A Crystal Set

Wirelesses were just being thought of. We

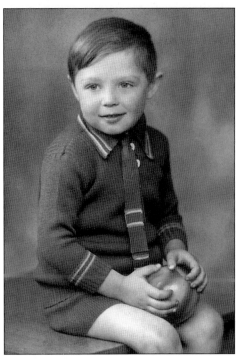

Charles Frederick Lord aged eight in 1938. Fred was named after his grandfather, Charles Frederick Moore, with whom his family lived for a while.

Jeanne Margerison (née Nixon) aged eight in 1934, at the time she was a pupil at Moorside primary school in Droylsden, where eventually she became a teacher.

had one very clever teacher. He taught the boys to make a radio. We could all listen and we all queued up, the whole school. You couldn't hear nothing, only 'Wow, wow, wow'. I said, 'It's lovely'. The boys hooked lines across the classroom: that was the aerial for it.

Vera Worth

St Mary's

The headmistress was Miss Frith, a sort of typical Victorian lady, very, very smart and stern. I remember when we first went there, it seems strange now, but they had small cots; they were like army cots but only low for the infants to sleep on. The hall was divided with high doors that you could pull across. About eleven o'clock, after everybody had milk, then they used to pull the doors across and all the infants used to get down on these cots and have an hours sleep, to refresh themselves for the afternoon. St Mary's only went up to age seven and from seven to eleven years you went to Moorside.

Fred Lord

Sh Sh Sh

When I was four, I went to St Mary's Church of England School. We had beds and we had to lie down in the afternoon for half an hour. We all had our own blanket and pillow. Along the wall was a frieze with pockets in and you had a symbol. You had to put your spare shoes, your handkerchief and your lunch in each pocket. My pillow and blanket had the Union Jack on and that was my symbol. The teacher used to sit in this chair rocking backwards and forwards going 'Sh sh sh' to get you all off to sleep. In that class I learnt my catechism because we were getting ready for being confirmed at St Mary's. We were taught the first psalm there: 'Blessed is the man that walketh not in the counsel of the ungodly', and that always stuck with me. I can remember the cream and the green paint which seemed to be standard during the war, a picture of the King on the wall and also 'The Boyhood of Raleigh' in the hallway.

Dorothy Clinton

School Outings

I remember one school trip we went to Morecambe. I was only small. I remember trading a camera for 1s 6d, because this poor lad was absolutely broke. I went to the chemist's to get a film put in and when he told me how much it was, I said, 'I can't afford that' and he had to take the flipping thing out again.

Betty Slater

London

I went to Lumb Lane. When I was aged eleven and in the top class in May 1967, we had a two-day trip to London, which was the first time it had ever been done. They did actually do it again, so perhaps we weren't that bad. There were three teachers shepherding fifty children. None of us would stay in our rooms: we wanted pillow fights. So at four o'clock in the morning, the poor headmaster had to get up and take us all for a walk on Clapham Common!

Kate Kerry

New Ideas

I went to Moorside about 1971. It was a period when they were advocating having a free day and letting children find their own level and having no structured teaching. You got a lot of creative work done by the children that wanted to do it but the ones that didn't want to do it, felt left out. We've had horizontal

Standard II at Poplar Street day school in Audenshaw in 1923 with their head teacher Mr Armitage and teacher Mrs Frostick. On the front row first on the left is Vera Worth (née Chapman).

A class at St Mary's church day school in Droylsden around 1947. On the third row from the back first on the left is Dorothy Clinton (née Worthington).

grouping, three different years of children in the one class, working with another class, so that one teacher would take the top age group for something, while you took the second age group for something else. It was a nightmare doing the timetable. In some ways it worked very well having older children with younger ones. They settled in quite easily. Some of them had got older brothers and sisters in the same class.

Jeanne Margerison

Brand New

Aldwyn County primary opened in 1953 as an infants' and juniors' school. I taught in the junior school. We all assembled the first day and hadn't been in many minutes, when the door opened and in walked an HMI, coming round to check that everything was going alright. I was a bit frightened, because it was my first day. There were just six classes, when it opened, a very small number of children, because we had to wait while the estate grew on the Moss. We had lovely playing fields, which were quite unique in those days. Schools had playgrounds. We had this lovely football field. It was very nice surroundings: windows all down one side of every classroom and so it was light and airy.

The infants and the juniors were joined by the dining room in those days and the school meals were cooked on the premises, which again was most unusual. It was still the days, when the container meals were taken out. We had absolutely wonderful school dinners.

We did take a party to see the Queen Mother, who came to Audenshaw Grammar in 1959, and we trailed children across to see her. We stood on Stamford Road. It was a very hot day. I'm sure somebody had a nose bleed!

I was there for about thirteen years, enough to see it build up and get to be a two form entry, because all those houses on Sunnyside in Droylsden were built.

Margaret Walker

Moving On

In the 1920s, every Monday morning during my last three years at Poplar Street, all our class walked though the fields and through a farmyard, until we came out onto Stamford Road and then we had to go to Lumb Lane, the council school, one full day a week. One term we had cookery, one term housekeeping and another laundry. We were making cakes and the teacher used to say, 'Put so much flour in' and we'd think, 'Ooh, we'll have a big cake. We'll put more flour in!', not realising there wasn't enough fat to make it. I used to say, 'Mam, can I eat it when I'm coming home?' She used to say, 'Yes. We don't want it here! Get it eaten!' The boys used to come home with us and they used to say, ' What have you made this week?' They used to say it tasted terrible but always wanted more next week! The boys were taught woodwork and at the end of term

A class at Aldwyn County Primary School on Aldwyn Park Road in 1958. The head teacher is Mr Taylor and the teacher is Miss Margaret Walker, who also describes her schooldays at Fairfield High School.

Dorothy Lord (née Vardy), aged eleven in 1939, in her Fairfield High School uniform, where she attended between 1939 and 1945.

would proudly carry home little stools, pipe racks and other things they had made.

Vera Worth

Scholarship Girl

I passed and went to Fairfield in the 1930s as a non-paying pupil: I think I was called a scholarship girl. Books were available second hand at a small charge for our use. At the term end the books were handed in and new second hand books issued at a reduced price. Our school clothes had to be covered by a letter of authorisation from the headmistress. My impressions – very strict, no nonsense, self-discipline, self control, walk single file on corridors and stairs, no running, emphasis on

being lady-like. There was punishment after school for any misdemeanour, pages of 'I must not …' written fifty or more times. For example, we wore wool hats, even in summer. I removed mine with the heat, was seen and severely reprimanded. I had to stay after school on three occasions and write 'I must not … ' many, many times.

Dorothy Lord

Hobson's Choice

In the 1930s I went across the road to Poplar Street, when I was eleven. I sat the Hobson exams to go to the grammar school. I got certain marks and I was in line for the Hobson grant. Because my father said that he was earning so much money and somebody else's father said that he was only earning so much, the other boy was allowed to have the place. I had to find somewhere else. So we chose Ashton Technical College, which was on Old Street at the back of what is now the library.

Harry Slater

Fairfield

My father decided that we should all go to Fairfield and so we all went, Brenda, Pat and Jacqueline. I went in 1941, when I was eleven. I didn't pass any examination: my father paid £16, I think, a term: we had to take it in the first day. We had air raid shelters on the hockey field. We used to have food always there, kept as emergency rations, in a little cubby hole near the door.

Betty Slater

Driving a Mistress Mad

The uniform was during the war these horrible dresses, like a rayony material, square necked with piping. They'd no shape. The rest was gymslips and these square necked blouses. We had woolly hats to start with, and then they were changed to berets, and a navy gaberdine. The forms were U, F and H, which was short for 'the Utmost For the Highest'. There were four houses, Rose, Shamrock, Daffodil and Thistle, representing the four countries. On each national day that particular house took the assembly. So if it was April 23rd, it always was an assembly based very much on Shakespeare and English music. There were four house gardens by the tennis courts but they were disastrous, because nobody had any time to look after them.

I became Head Girl eventually. I had to go and get the head, Miss Bradley, for prayers and check that she was presentable. She used to stand up before you went down and say, 'Is my slip showing, Margaret?' You had to check all these little things for her and make the vote of thanks at the Speech Day, which was a bit impressive at the Houldsworth Hall in the afternoon on Deansgate, where Church House is now. We all had to wear our summer frocks and the governors sat on the platform. I suppose the feature was this 'Fairfield Silence', when two members of staff would walk down the sides of the aisles of the hall and a miraculous silence would fall on the assembled body.

Miss Bradley had a rhyme: I must say about the word 'wood', which is an old English word for 'mad':

Speech Day at Houldsworth Hall in Manchester in 1937. Fairfield High School pupils sit in rows alongside their families and teachers with Lena Slack, the pianist, seated with the music teacher and conductor, Miss Booth.

37

Lena Slack (née Johnson) as head girl in 1938-1939, near the 'New Extension', which was being built onto the original building at Fairfield High School for Girls.

'Never say we're sat; never say we're stood.
For the sound of that drives a mistress wood.
If you must, use English that is fitting.
Always say 'We're standing, we're seated or
we're sitting.'

If you did an essay and it wasn't right, you'd have to say that for her to get it into your mind, to get your correct grammar.

Miss Brooks used to teach us for Maths as well. We reckoned she used to start off with Mental Arithmetic, as she was coming down the corridor. She used to be muttering it as she walked in the door and she used to say, 'Answer, please!' and we'd be thinking, 'What'd she say?'

Margaret Walker

Name on the Honours Board

Whilst I was at Fairfield [1967-1972], we had the 175th anniversary. We went down to Manchester Cathedral in the morning to have a service. At night, the school was open and there were all sorts of displays on. My friend and I were doing French peasant dancing in the hall, set out with tables and umbrellas, like a French café. Another group did German dancing and there was Moravian dancing.

Miss Gleave was the headmistress. She always brought her dog, Prince, a Shetland Sheep dog, to school with her. If we were very good, we were allowed to take him for a walk at lunchtime. He could be quite nasty. He snapped at one or two of the girls. He always used to lie on one of the *chaise longues* in her study.

I did do one naughty thing. I got my name on the Honours Board but only because I put it there! I did it with nail varnish. It was in the stone hall, where there was a very old grandfather clock with the sun and moon. They weren't always sure if it was me, because there was another girl with the same name as me. It was the age of miniskirts. We were supposed to be able to kneel on the floor and our hems were never to be more than 2 inches above the knee. My form teacher took it upon herself to take my hem down and make me sew it back up again. I sewed it in exactly the same place!

Kate Kerry

No Coupons

Just after the end of the war, a school camp was organized, the venue being the village of Rosslare in Southern Ireland. The local butcher and sweetshop owner got quite used to lads asking them to stand next to their wares to have a photo taken. Most of us had never seen sides of beef hung up or masses of sweets and chocolates laid out and available for anyone with the money – no coupons required!

John Lord

School Life

Less than half of the pupils had won county minor scholarships, which paid for fees and books. All other entrants had to pass an entrance examination. Some of the Audenshaw boys were helped by the Hobson Foundation, an old established charity, which either paid fees or bought the books. Uniform consisted of a blue blazer and cap, both with the school badge, grey trousers (short for a year or two), a grey pullover and long, grey stockings. When we first entered the school, we changed into plimsolls to protect the floor.

We didn't have much contact with the headmaster, 'Johnnie' Lord, who taught History. He presided over the morning assembly for the whole school in the gallery and the well of the hall, which also served as a gym, with its wall bars and climbing ropes. We played rugby, athletics and cricket on one afternoon a week and also Saturday morning games, supervised by the prefects and one member of staff. Games

Year IV of White House outside the new Utility building, housing the Biology Laboratory and a class room, at Audenshaw Grammar School for Boys in 1946. Second row from the front, kneeling first on the left, is George Walker.

The prefects of Audenshaw Grammar School for Boys in 1946. Centre front is the head teacher Mr John Lord, directly behind whom stands Arthur Bantoft.

competitions, involving the four houses, White, Blue, Green and Red, were keenly fought. The boys came from Audenshaw, Denton and Droylsden with a few from Ashton. There was no school transport and boys walked, cycled or caught a bus. Only 'Johnnie' Lord had a very battered car and managed to get enough petrol to keep it going all through the war.

In the Sixth Form as prefects we helped supervise the lower school in the yard and changing rooms and at break and taking detentions after school. The system allowed some corporal punishment, usually a slipper across the backside. I coached the Wilton House junior rugby team: the original four houses had been replaced by Wilton, Derby, Assheton and Holland, plus Clarendon and Stamford, named after local landed gentry.

Arthur Bantoft

CHAPTER 3
At Work

Horses and carts carrying goods past St Stephen's church in the early 1900s. Stockport Road runs across the foreground with Guide Lane just visible on the left and Audenshaw Road on the right.

By Horse and Cart

In the early 1900s, my grandfather, George Beesley, was the coachman for Amos Davies, who was managing the firm of Robert Noblett, leather dresser. Grandfather Beesley drove four horse-drawn vehicles for the family and had two horses, which were stabled at the bottom of the yard. For family occasions there was a wagonette and a phaeton. When only Mr Davies went out, he was driven in a dog cart.

The other vehicle was called a tub, a round cart used for the delivery each day of parcels of leathers to the numerous hat factories in Denton. If he returned from the Blue Pig on Saturday nights a little the worse for wear, he would insist that grandma accompanied him down the yard to make sure that the horses were properly settled for the night. A case of putting the horse before the wife!

Arthur Bantoft

Charles Frederick Moore, Fred Lord's grandfather, after whom he was named. He operated a haulage business from Droylsden, conveying goods as far afield as Manchester.

Trading

In the late 1920s, we lived with my grandfather, who had a haulage business. He began with a horse and cart he kept at the back of the Palace cinema and he moved on to a Bedford flat lorry afterwards. My grandfather traded as 'Charles Frederick Moore' in the business of groceries. He'd pick up rolls of wool and cloth at the mills in Droylsden and take them down to Manchester. In the holidays, I used to travel with my uncle Fred [Moore], who drove the lorry, and I'd go down with him. We'd drop the cloth off and then we'd go into Manchester and we'd pick up sides of bacon, full cheeses and all sorts of goods and we'd

distribute them on the way home back to Droylsden at various grocers' shops. I always remember most of those wholesalers in those days were in the basements of the bigger buildings in Manchester and the aroma from the bacon and the coffee that were under there, years and years of aroma building up, was absolutely wonderful.

Fred Lord

The Smithy

It was just after Shepley Road. When we first went to our sweet shop in the 1950s, people used to bring the horses to be shoed.

An advertisement of 1931 for Leonard Hartley, who ran several grocer's shops, including one on Guide Lane, where he brought his horses to the nearby smithy.

It stood back from the road between the houses and the cake shop. Children, Saturday morning chiefly, used to come along with their horses. There used to be one or two people that had horses pulling the delivery trucks: Leonard Hartley round the corner on Guide Lane had a grocer's shop; he always pulled his truck with horses. It used to scare me to death, when he pulled up outside Granny Green's. Getting a bit worried about the traffic passing, the horse used to be going on. I'd be in the front room round the corner there with this blessed horse going by.

Joan Jebb

Shoeing

Not quite opposite to Guide Lane Methodists', Harry Law had this smithy. He used to make carts and mend cart wheels. He also did the shoeing on the horses.

Harry Slater

Wallers and Watermen

According to the 1871 Census my great grandfather, Isaac Johnson, lived in what was then Dick Lane and he was sixty then. He was a stonewaller and my grandfather, his son Adam, twenty-two at the time of the census, was also employed by the Manchester Corporation Waterworks department. He did some stone walling but was employed as a waterman. They gave lodging to the navvies, who worked on the reservoirs. They must all have been lodging with my great grandfather's family.

Lena Slack

On the left is the site of the smithy on Guide Lane in the 1960s. It lay almost opposite Guide Lane Wesleyan Methodist church.

Fred Langridge with his son Eric behind their home on Watergate behind Ryecroft Hall around 1940. One of his sons, David, recounts how his father was the lamp lighter for Audenshaw, after being caretaker at the YMCA.

A Good Flagger

I remember that in the 1950s Roy had a very good flagger called Jack Derwent, and he lived in those houses near the grammar school. He used to always work without any shirt on in the summer and he had this brown skin and black hair. I always thought he was like a gypsy but he was the best flagger out of every council that Roy [Audenshaw's borough surveyor] had known. He never found one that wobbled when Jack had done it.

Frances Conneely

Knocking-up and Lamp Lighting

I do remember in the 1930s the early morning noises of people wearing clogs going to the different factories around and the knocker-up coming and knocking at people's windows: he got paid a few coppers by the people for that. Of course we knew it was morning, when the lamp lighters were knocking about, even with our curtains shut, because we could hear them at the lamps turning them off. In the evening we'd wait for them to light up so that we could go and play around the lamp-post. We played plenty of games in the streets, because there was no traffic at all.

Bill Pollitt

Clock Lamps

Really for a long time, right up to the war, my father was a lamp lighter. At the corner of the street they had what they called clock lamps which have a pilot light on and an automatic wind up mechanism. My father had to wind it up, I think it was only once a week, to keep the thing ticking and these lamps would go on and off automatically. Also he had to keep these lamps in good repair, so that, if any glass sheets were broken, he would have to repair these. He had to clean them and with the clock lamps he would have to alter the clock setting about once every month to make it earlier or later. With the lamp lighting stick he had to clean it out every night because you got deposits on the gas ways. He had to fill the valve at the bottom with a carbide, which was an evil smelling material, and water dripping onto the carbide emits the gas which gave off the light. We had big tins of carbide in the house which each carried about five pounds. Very useful stuff for taking little pebbles away and putting in the ink well at school which caused the ink to bubble up and caused quite a mess. You never did it on your own ink well! I think three or four lamp lighters were employed by the council for the whole of Audenshaw.

David Langridge

Miners

Father was a collier at the Snipe and at Bradford. He always said it was hard work and he didn't want either me or Bill to go into it. Sometimes he said he'd be kneeling all day, many times in water; the seam was that low and it was wet all day. He had pads on his

Henry Reece who was a coal miner at the Snipe Pit on Ashton Moss and later at Bradford Colliery, in his garden at Angel Street, Denton, with his wife Margaret and his granddaughter Jean Travis, in the late 1930s.

The family of Henry (Harry) Reece, whose children recall his days as a coal miner, in the early 1900s. Back row, on the left is Doris and on the right Elizabeth (Lizzie), while at the front on the left is Margaret and on the right Tom.

knees and he used to wear drawers, he called them, and they used to be wet through with sweat, when he brought them home. He'd come home on the tram, his face all black, all his clothes black. He'd wash himself, his hair and that and then we'd have to rub his back down for him in front of the fire.

Tom and Bill Reece

Life Underground

Dad's [Harry Reece] back had blue marks all over, where he'd been hit by the coal. He used to wear a little skull cap and they went down

45

the pit on a little… , they used to call it a 'horse' – like a clog sole with leather on the top. One rail went down and they'd go down there. It was about one mile underneath, where they'd work, from where the cage took them down. Coming back it was all up-hill and he had a walking stick then to help him get back up. They used to hide their cigarettes and matches, before they went into the pit, to have a smoke, so they could have them ready for when they came out. They used to chew tobacco.

Mabel Lawson

Mr Birch

Our next door neighbour worked at the local pit. I used to be terrified of meeting Mr Birch in the back entry, when he was coming home from work. With his face all black with coal dust, just his pink lips and the whites of his eyes standing out from the black mask, he frightened me to death, although he was really the gentlest of men. There were no pithead baths in those days, and he would banish all the children from the kitchen and take his bath in front of the fire.

Lena Slack

The Tripe Works

My mother worked at a tripe works, Hulme's, on Denton Road, at the back of where the community centre is now, where was once St Hilda's church. They had a shop in Denton but this was where they cleaned it and got it all ready for shops. She worked for Hulme's for a long while; I bet she was over seventy. She had to clean the bellies of cows. I never touch

tripe me because I saw it in the raw in the factory. It was very hot and steamy in these big tubs all round with bellies in.

Rose Perfect

The Jam Works

My mother first went strawberry picking at Robertson's in the war, when we were very young, to earn extra money and she was there thirty years. You just take the stalk off. You get paid so much per tray, with so many pounds in a tray. The seeds used to go down the nails and make them sceptic. It wasn't very pleasant but there was a lot of camaraderie because the same people went back for the strawberry season every year. Some were kept on; Mum was. It lasted only about a month, five weeks at the most, because it was just English strawberries and perhaps a few Scottish ones. The jam was made fresh and preserved just in season whereas now they freeze them. The jars have to be sterilised. At one time you used to be able to take jars back and get a penny on every jar. You got a lot of children doing that but then health and safety rules came in. If they were chipped at all it was dangerous; so they stopped that and they bought all new glass. In fact, they were stacked in pallets of, perhaps, two hundred on a pallet. If a pallet fell over every one would be scrapped; they wouldn't risk any glass going into the product at all. The boiling house was very, very hot, where the boiling pans were. That was fascinating to see all the ingredients going in, all the fresh fruit and the sugar. Sugar is the main ingredient: they must use about forty tons of sugar a day in a huge vat. The lemon curd is made with real eggs. At one time you used to see them breaking the eggs but then they bought in liquid, fresh egg.

The bottling part was very noisy because all the jars were coming round crashing against one another as they came from the washer. It all came down a huge band, all this jam coming to the end and people carrying it off into pallets, the labels already on.

Dorothy Clinton

Housework

We just had a paraffin lamp. You sat round your table if you wanted to do or write anything, near the lamp in the middle. We used to scrub the front every Friday night, everyone around washing their doorstep right to the edge of the pavement. It was jolly hard work. We used a brown and white donkey stone.

Wash day was hard work with the dolly tub and a posser (a contraption with a metal base and a wooden handle that was used to pound clothes). You'd start about nine o'clock. It was two o'clock when you'd finished and then you had to put them out. You had a boiler; you had to get your fire going, heat your water before you could start washing. You'd generally two dolly tubs and your posser or your peggy. You'd turn it with the peggy, or up and down with the posser.

Ruth Rogerson

Wash Day

In the 1930s we went into a two-up and two-down terrace. No bathroom, no hot water, a small yard leading to a communal entry and

The delivery van of Hough's, tripe dresser, at Hooley Hill, Audenshaw, in front of Shelmerdine's firm which serviced hat makers in Denton and the area. Behind lies the firm of Sam Ainsworth, who made hat bodies, and on the left is Richmond Street with the entrance to the Wilton Engine Company.

an outside toilet in the yard. Conditions were hard. There was a black fireplace range, water to be heated and lino floors. Rugs were actually made by hand. They were pegged from old coats, which we cut up and they were pegged onto sacking. There were no carpets. My father and mother colour-washed the walls with yellow ochre. There were several colours; I remember green, a yellow and a mauve, and you mixed this powder with cold water and actually applied it on the walls with a small sponge or alternatively a rag. This brightened up the place to a degree and it was quite pretty.

The food was basic, rabbit, oxtail, 'skirt' for potato pie, cow's heart were casseroled with onion for nourishment. Rice and sago

Dorothy Clinton as a girl with her brother Keith and her mother May Worthington, who worked at Robertson's Jam Works. This photograph was taken in the early 1940s, to send to her father, who was serving in the army.

pudding, sometimes dumpling, a jam roly-poly, if there was a little extra money. Clothes were bought sparingly for a weekly few pence from a clothing shop. This slowly mounted until a coat could be bought. The children wore hand-me-downs from one child to the next. Warm clothing was patched and repaired and socks were darned. My grandmother made many dresses for us from material scraps and by cutting up her old dresses and making up, especially for me, as I was the eldest. Knitting, sewing, crotchet were taught by my grandmother.

People cleaned their small homes. Ours was spotless but basic, for existence only.

Washday was a full day of heating a copper boiler with a small fire underneath to boil clothes. The clothes were then placed in a dolly tub by wooden tongs, soap added and then ponched. The poncher was a pole with a three-legged base or a pole with a metal base with holes in it, so that, when ponched, the water would swirl up and over the clothes in a beating action. They were always clean when finished. Then followed rinsing, dolly blue for whitening the white clothes and starching and then mangling with heavy rollers. Ironing was by heavy irons placed on the gas cooker rings, first for heating or by placing by the hot coals in the grate. As one iron was being used, a spare one was already heating to take its place. Emptying the dolly tub was by the back yard grid; then we filled buckets from the cold water tap – very physical and tiring work. Ironing was actually done in those days on a blanket, which was spread on the table, which was used for meals, and then covered with an old sheet. There weren't any ironing boards. Washing was hung and dried in our narrow, little back yard. Washing lines were close together through lack of space. It was an effort to avoid the length of washing, if one ventured into the yard. On washing day, kitchens were full of steam and washing was also hung on racks near the ceiling to dry. The racks were hoisted up and down by a rope to enable filling them and then raised to dry.

Steps were scrubbed and donkey stoned. Back yards were swilled with water. Black grates were polished with Zebo – a thick, black polish put on by brush and rubbed, until it gleamed. Rugs were shaken outside, floors swept by brush and cinders and ash removed from grates, The cinders were retained for the next day and used on top of coals, so as to last longer. Thrift was paramount – the peelings from vegetables were also put on top of the coals to enable the fire to last longer.

Dorothy Lord

The Undertakers

There was a little triangular piece of garden with a form, by Pike's Funeral Undertaker's, on Guide Lane. The old men used to sit on this form and they used to say that Mr Pike used to stare at them through the window and size them up ready! The window was painted halfway up with his name on it and you could just see him with his glasses looking over.

Bill Pollitt

Carrying the Coffin

My father used to carry the coffin for Zachariah Pike, the undertaker's, joiner's and builder's. He had to wear black, a black suit, and used to have to wear a hat, like a silk hat. He got 2s 6d if he just carried but, if he walked at the front of the hearse, he got an extra 6d. He was walking down Guide Lane one day

Gladys Vardy, mother of Dorothy Lord, in the late 1920s. Dorothy describes the tedious and harsh routine of housework, and the economies adopted during the Depression and the war by her mother and family.

with the hat on, in front of the hearse, and a little lad ran in to his mother and said, 'There's a carnival outside. I've just seen Mr Slater walking in the carnival!'

Harry Slater

Life in a Cotton Mill

My mother did tell me that soon after they first came to live at Droylsden in 1904, she thought, 'What's that noise every morning?' Of course it was the noise of the people going past to the mill [in their clogs]. Somebody asked her if she would like to go and work in the mill; they would get her a job. When she told my father, he said, 'Oh, no way!' Anyway she did go, Oakfield Mill, I think. She only worked one day and she couldn't close her eyes that night. She said everytime she tried to close her eyes, she could see the machinery going up and down weaving. She never attempted it again.

Jeanne Margerison

A Spinner

In the 1920s my father used to complain how the threads were constantly breaking, of the poor quality of the cotton and how he had to run about from end to end in his pair of mules. As a minder he was an aristocrat of the job, having moved up from a little piecer to a big piecer, to a joiner spinner, finally a spinner, padding with great agility across oil soaked floors in his bare feet.

Lena Slack

Talking With Your Hands

I've worked at Christy's in Droylsden in the office, in the 1960s. You went into the building through a gatehouse. There was a little reception office on the right but you could drive in and the buildings went around this open square. The office I was in looked down into this square, but of course we had to go to take a message or go and see somebody in the mill. You didn't stay in the weaving room very long: the noise was horrendous. I knew a lot of people that talked with their hands and exaggerated what they were saying, because they'd worked in the mill.

Jeanne Margerison

Christy's Mill

In 1948, I went with a party of Sixth Form

The firm of Z. Pike & Sons on Guide Lane on the corner of Paradise Street in the 1940s. They were joiners, builders and funeral directors.

girls from Fairfield High School to inspect Christy's mill in Droylsden. We were led up a well-worn spiral staircase to the dining room. Christy's was an old-established mill and was one of the first in the country to make the 'Royal Turkish Towelling' for which it is famous. For when Queen Victoria saw a sample at the Crystal Palace Exhibition in 1852, she was so pleased that she allowed Christy's to use this name. First we saw the bales of raw cotton being broken up and cleaned. Although it is an old mill, many of the machines are the latest models. We watched the cotton through every stage from the raw material to the finished towels. It was first cleaned, then spun and dyed and woven. In the weaving shed we saw that many towels were being made for export: names were being woven in the towels for such concerns as Cunard, White Star Line and the New Zealand Railway Company, on a Jacquard machine.

The noise of the machinery was a drawback, for in some rooms only the people directly next to our guide could hear. After a time the employees get used to it, and soon learn to converse by lip-reading, although after working for many years some people become deaf. On entering one room, we were met by a stifling heat, and one girl in the room was working in her bare feet on a concrete floor. Not long ago, most of the people used to work like this.

Beryl Kershaw

Jones' Sewing Machine Works

My grandfather Adam Andrew and my mother Jean lived in Glasgow and my grandfather worked at Singer Sewing machine works and he came down here to be

An advertisment produced in 1951 in the centenary booklet of Christy's Ltd, advertising the Royal Turkish towels for which the firm was famous.

manager at Jones' in the 1880s. He worked there until he died about 1914.

Margaret Slater

Hard Work Polishing

I went to Jones' in about 1915: I worked there for three and a half years. I was in the French polishing, the woodwork part. The tables that the machines fit on, that's the part I worked on polishing. All the woodwork came from Canada and it was packed in grey cotton wool and it used to eat into the varnish. We had to rub and rub until we got all that out. It was jolly hard work.

Ruth Rogerson

An advertisement for Jones' Sewing Machine Company, off Guide Lane, in the early 1900s, entitled 'Busy' and 'Home from School'.

The Leather Works

My dad worked at Noblett's, the leather dressers. He used to cut the leather ready for going into the hat to shape the hat inside and he eventually became foreman cutter. There was a house that went with that. In the 1950s I went to work at Noblett's in the warehouse. I put a decorative mark on the leather and then packed them. The mark was done with a heated roller from a gas jet and you ran the leather under the roller. You counted it in grosses, a hundred and forty-four. It was a very big, long room and you went up the stairs to it. There was a very big clock with an arm on it and you chose your number and pushed it in to clock in: it registered the time when you got in to work. There was a very, very long room with racks of all these different shades of hat leathers in; you can't imagine the number of different shades of leather there are. It had

to be shaded and a gross of leathers had to be more or less all the same shade, so that in itself was a job.

It came in as raw leather, like a chamois leather; it smelt terrible. It was rolled and dried and they used to cut it from these huge skins. They brought it into the finishing warehouse, where it had this line more or less burnt along it, just one line. Sometimes it was stamped out with a pattern, and that was a big iron machine. You had to pull a lever down onto it, get it dead centre. Woe betide if you made a mistake, because they were really expensive things that you were dealing with.

At Lumb Lane side, that's where all the leathers came in and were stretched and dried over that side. Then they came in to the other side, just behind the Blue Pig. You never went in the office, you had to knock on the door and it would flop up. Then there was a private room where they had a board meeting; you crept past there.

Dorothy Clinton

Amos Davies

The other side of the Blue Pig, in Brookfield Street, was Amos Davies' leatherworks and they did the same sort of work as Noblett's, which was hat leathers for inside gentlemen's hats, in conjunction with the Denton hatting. My sister worked at Amos Davies' and my husband's father was manager after Amos himself died. Ernest Slack he was called. Well it went out of business about 1939-1940, taken over by Applebly's, as a rabbit skin factory, and it has now been pulled down.

Lena Slack

Robert Noblett

Amos Davies was managing the firm of Robert Noblett, until the son, Robert junior, was of age. Part ran alongside Lumb Lane and there were buildings at the bottom of Noblett's yard. Amos Davies lived in a house halfway down the yard. Later, when Robert took over, he acquired the small factory on the opposite side of Lumb Lane on land now used as a small park.

Arthur Bantoft

The workers of Amos Davies, leather dresser, outside his works on Brookfield Street, by the Blue Pig, in Audenshaw, in the early 1900s. Lena Slack's grandfather, Ernest Slack, the work's manager, is first on the left in the back row. At the front on the right first is Nellie Worthington, aunt to Dorothy Clinton, sitting next to Annie Slack, sister to Ernest.

Lena Slack's grandparents, Ernest and Florence Slack, on their wedding day, outside their home at No. 430, Audenshaw Road, in the early 1900s. Ernest was work's manager at Amos Davies', leather dresser, off Audenshaw Road.

No Talking

In 1904, my mother, Annie Beesley, aged thirteen, began work at Dedman's factory near St Hilda's church. They made wash leathers from the skins of hides used to make leathers for the hat trade. Each night skins were hung in a top floor room. A hot brick was put into a cauldron of sulphur and then the room was closed for the night. In the morning, the first job of the girls was to rush in and open the windows, to emerge with streaming eyes and gasping for breath from the poisonous and corrosive gas. Mr Dedman worked in the same room as the girls and imposed a regime of strict silence. When mother later went to work at Noblett's in 1909, the first sound she heard was the workers singing, 'One Man Went To Mow'. She thought she was in heaven!

Arthur Bantoft

Dreadful Smell

We went down Pitt Street and there was Appleby's Bunny Works we called it, and this was where, on a hot day, if the door was open, the pong was horrible and you could see all these rabbit skins hung up

Annie Beesley, mother of Arthur Bantoft around 1910. She lived in one of the old cottages, dated 1793, near the Blue Pig and worked at Dedman's factory, where they made wash leathers.

drying. Before you got there you went past Peter Blyth's and I can smell it today: it smelled of glue and cardboard.

Fred Clark

Making Boxes

I went to Peter Blyth's box making in Pitt Street and I stayed there until 1934. I was there nearly twenty years. Cardboard comes in great big packs. First of all, when you got an order, say for a dozen (it could go up to a thousand), you got a box for a dozen, blouse boxes we'll say. You had to work out how many boxes you could get out of a sheet of cardboard: how many pieces of cardboard you would need. It was interesting work. Hat boxes was another section but I wasn't in it. Christmas was always a busy time.

Ruth Rogerson

George Blyth, President of the YMCA for 1911-1912, ran a box-making business at Victoria Works on Pitt Street, off Guide Lane. The firm called 'Peter Blyth's' made especially boxes for the hat trade.

The Box Shop

My father's mother was a Downs of Downs' Box Shop. The girls of the family never inherited, only the boys and men. So they were the rich side of my father's family. It started off near Bye Street, further down Paradise Street in a little two-up two-down shop. This was Julius, my dad's grandpa. They had a very big, like a removal van, pulled by a horse, to cart the boxes about, chiefly for the hatting industry. As time went on, they knocked down one or two of the houses, making it a bit bigger, until they had the whole of Providence Street on the left-hand side, with the offices at the end and the factory further down.

Joan Jebb

All Kinds of Boxes

I started work at Julius Downs on Guide Lane, corner of Providence Street. I worked there until Eileen was born. We made mostly huge boxes. They were for foreigners, because we couldn't understand the labels we had to put on. They were for material being sent from England, in Chinese writing. We made little chocolate boxes and big hat boxes. I loved it. I worked there for more than twelve years. My first week's wage was 7s 6d and I ran all the way home to give it to my mother: I was so proud. It had to close down: the building wasn't substantial and we moved to Denton in about 1930, opposite Denton Station, where Sainsbury's is now. I had to walk the full length from

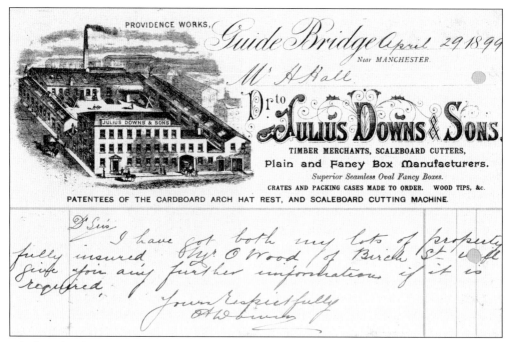

The letter heading in 1899 of Julius Downs, who ran a box making business from Providence Works on Providence Street, off Guide Lane. He later moved to premises in Denton and, like Peter Blyth, he produced boxes mainly for the hat trade.

here, twice a day to Sainsbury's along Corporation Road and in the winter when there was snow!

Vera Worth

Making the Hat Bodies

My father's firm was in Richmond Street, Hooley Hill. The firm was S.D. Ainsworth & Son. My father was the son and Samuel Ainsworth was my grandfather, who started the firm. My father had about twelve work-people and they made the hat body and it came out like a felt cone, very flat. It started off with you feeding out the bags of tight cotton wool (he made the wool hats) onto a moving belt, which took it up through a machine. At the other end it came out like a web, a very gentle web, beautiful, and they guided this over revolving cones. When they got enough layers on, they would cut through the centre with shears and you would have two beautifully soft cone-shaped hats. They had ladies weighing them: they had to be the exact weight. If they weren't, they would get an extra piece of this web coming through, layer it on top of it or take a layer off. Then it went to be hardened. The men were hardeners. They put a piece of canvas the shape of the cone, flat, in the centre of the hat and they had a machine that pulled, like a great big iron, that was also covered with material. That was the hot one and they pulled it down and the cloth went in wet and all the steam used to come out and then it came out like felt. They lifted the press up and, when it came out, it was like a felt cone. That was what they sold. When I was a little girl, I used to go. It was run by a great big boiler outside, where they shovelled coal into it all the time, and all done with steam. The engine was always started up with a big belt being put onto these two wheels and at the end they used to snap that off to stop them going round and stop the engine.

It was closed, when the hatting went down: it was always very spasmodic. My father had a car, which not many people had then. When work came, he had to go and round the people up, if he had a big order. He had to go in the car and tell

them there was work again. When my grandfather died, my father modernised it, put an electric motor in. With the war those sort of hats went downhill and they just fizzled out.

Mavis Langridge

Scott and Hodson's

My grandfather was foundry manager of Scott and Hodson's and my father was foreman moulder. The firm closed down in the '30s. It's where Mono Pumps is now. They used to make huge flywheels. To get them out of the foundry, they used to have to take that huge, huge wall down on the side of the road and

Samuel Ainsworth, grandfather of Mavis Langridge and founder of the firm of S.D. Ainsworth & Son, in the early 1900s. He and his son Reg made hat bodies at their Richmond Works in Hooley Hill.

A flywheel in June 1931 ready for a mill at the foundry of Scott & Hodson, in Martin Street, where Mono Pumps is sited now. Fred Clark and Bessie Watt describe the work their grandfather and father carried out there.

build it all up again. The last big flywheel they made was supposed to be the biggest in the country, somewhere in Lincolnshire for an electricity place.

Bessie Watt

Flywheels

When the First World War broke out, Dad and his brothers were on war work. Instead of building flywheels, they were building mill engines. Dad often couldn't come home, because when they were casting, he had to be there all the time. So I used to take his tea. I knew the place quite well; down into Martin Street, there was a great big door that you went in into the yard. If that door was fast you went in the office way and you had to pass a check-in place, where they had these little check pass things. The yard was full of scrap metal. If you went down the yard, instead of going into the foundry, they had a line of toilets with no doors on. There must have been twelve I should think, and they were just seats all in the open. When you went into the foundry, I mean we were told all about hell at Sunday school, and I thought that's what that place was, hell, because it was full of dust and fumes and it smelt. My dad had a little office in the corner of the foundry. It had glass round two sides, and you could hardly see through the windows, because they were covered in this film of black dust. He had a big desk there and a tall seat, like you see in these offices. I could just about manage to climb up on the rungs and sit on there. Everything was covered in black dust. They had wooden patterns that used to come out the pattern shop. Then they put bricks round with all this black sand and then they put the metal in. I often wondered why my dad's suits were always full of holes and that was why; it was the molten metal that used to go on them. I remember him telling me there was hardly a week went past that he didn't have to send somebody down to Manchester Eye Hospital to have metal taken out of their eyes.

Normally they made the flywheels in four segments and they were bolted together. Dad once told me that, when his father was foundry foreman, they made a flywheel that big that it wouldn't come out through the door and they had to take a wall down to get it out. They used to have twelve horses with this stuff on there and they used to close the road off, because, he said, once they started going up the hill they couldn't stop, they daren't stop, because they would never be able to start again to go down to the left, down into the London North Western coal yard.

Fred Clark

Mono Pumps

In the 1960s I worked at Arnfield's at Guide Bridge in the office. It was Mono Pumps. That was the first time I'd had an electric typewriter, which was quite an innovation then. One of the offices I worked in was next to the machine shop and the noise was horrendous but you got used to it. They built

The table tennis team of General Gas Appliances of Corporation Road, Audenshaw, in 1948. They had won victories in various local leagues. The sketches are by A.E. Schofield, who was on the team. Second from the left (centre front), is David Langridge, who worked at the firm during the Second World War.

Delta Works on Groby Road, the firm of Austin Hopkinson and also known as Pikrose, which made machinery for the coal mining industry. This is the back view.

a new block and moved us out into this new block and nobody liked it, because it was so quiet! You could hear what anybody said. You couldn't talk about anybody!

Jeanne Margerison

Planet Foundry

My parents were not born in this area but came from Falkirk, Stirlingshire, in the mid '20s, when my father took a job in the pattern shop of Planet Foundry, later part of Allied Iron Founders', latterly Glynwed. A number of Scots came south as Falkirk was a chief light-iron casting district of the country, along with Coalbrookdale.

Christine Grimshaw

Crop Driers

I worked at General Gas on Corporation Road as a junior draughtsman in the 1940s in the drawing office. After the war, General

Gas went back to their normal work of designing gas cookers. They also made a lot of more complex things – crop driers, which became popular just after the war. They made industrial air heaters as well and they made gas fires. General Gas closed down in the 1970s but I'd already left there.

David Langridge

Delta Works (Pikrose)

My father worked at Pikrose from the 1930s for over forty years. Basically he was a mining engineer: he became a foreman and later on he was involved with sales. He was a district engineer much of the time and so he was very often on the road. He covered an area, which stretched as far as Stoke-on-Trent, all of Staffordshire. There were a lot of mines of course in those days that he visited. Pikrose was known as concerned with coal cutting machinery. Such a machine was invented by Austin Hopkinson, who started off the firm. The exterior was always an ivy-covered building and there was a hedge going round.

There was a cricket field in front. It was a very attractive building and exterior.

Brenda Tunstall

Austin Hopkinson

John started working at Pikrose, when he was fourteen, in about 1926, as an apprentice. You had to do seven years. As an engineer, he did coal cutting machinery. He used to go out with Brenda's dad. They used to go to Wales a lot. Austin Hopkinson looked after his workpeople. His profits were divided between the men. Then they had sick pay. It wasn't a union place at all. He didn't believe in the unions and you didn't need to argue with him, because he was kind. I remember the apprentices 'coming out'. The older men had told them to go on strike for more money. They were that innocent, they didn't know what a strike was. Three of them went out. Austin Hopkinson went up to them, as he was coming out, and he said to them: 'You're supposed to be inside. What are you doing here?' They said, 'We're on strike'. He said, 'Never mind on strike!' They had another one and when they all went back on the Monday, he'd disappeared. He'd closed the gates and he didn't come back for about six weeks. They couldn't work and they were glad to see him, when he came back. So he was firm in that sense; he was a kind man.

When you worked there, it was a job for life. When he died, Austin Voorsanger ran it for him and he was good. Austin Hopkinson more or less adopted him as a son.

Florence Dyson

Florence Dyson's husband John, who worked at Pikrose, on one of his assignments.

Austin Voorsanger

Austin Voorsanger's father was Austin Hopkinson's batman in the war and he brought him up from a boy. When he was sixteen, he went into the firm: he started right at the bottom. He took him through the firm and he became Managing Director. He was Dutch originally.

Brenda Tunstall

Couldn't You Have Waited?

My grandma's sister was married to the gentleman who owned the brickworks, Jimmy Harrison. Jackson's got one at Denton, that one in Audenshaw, one in Adswood, about five I think. Uncle Jim Harrison, although he was well-to-do, he'd still got a Lancashire accent: he didn't put on airs and graces like to the men; 'What's doing, lad?' he say. One of the men was driving his Rolls Royce and he skidded in Stockport and he hit the front door of a bank and broke it off. Oh, he went in fear and trembling, with his cap in his hand, twiddling it round. He thought Uncle Jim would say, 'You're sacked: get your cards: you're finished.' He said, 'What were tha' trying to do? Couldn't tha've waited until it opened?'

Bessie Watt

Caretakers

I was born in the YMCA at 36, Denton Road, Audenshaw, in the late 1920s. My parents were the caretakers there. It wasn't paid service but they had free accommodation. So our house had a door opening out to the YMCA internally, and we used to have two bedrooms upstairs. Downstairs we just had the front room, which had a little hole in the wall, like a serving hatch, which actually came onto the library and behind that, a door which led to the main building of the YMCA. We had a kitchen and dining room at the back of the house. There was also an outside toilet which, of course, was an outside tippler, a small yard which opened up into a huge area and then the back of the YMCA. There were steps down to a cellar where there was some bathing accommodation. The first room we came to was the library and then there were small rooms, committee rooms; we would go upstairs where there was a big billiard room with three full size billiard tables. My parents had a little shop where they sold sweets and they made Oxo. I remember my mother started to make this Oxo and one of the lads saying 'It's too strong, Mrs Langridge'. She put one Oxo cube in and I think she charged about 2d. She'd think not of putting less than that in because it was such a huge profit. But eventually she used one Oxo cube for two cups.

David Langridge

Ryecroft Hall

My grandparents were caretakers at Ryecroft Hall. Mum and dad had their wedding reception in there and grandma, being the sort of person who could get anyone to do anything, managed to get the council to lay on flowers and a fountain. I believe mum and dad's wedding reception was something to be seen but of course I wasn't there. Grandma's was a live-in-job. There were three bedrooms. Grandma's was enormous. Mum's was the second biggest: there was a double bed in it and wardrobes and miles and miles of space. Auntie Vera's was, I would imagine, the box room, which was halfway down the stairs. I always remember there was pink polka dot wallpaper in it – revolting! At the very back we had a very big kitchen: it was the main room that grandma lived in and it always had a Chesterfield suite and the walls had panelling on originally. Then you went out into a little, square hall and the front door was there, and then to the right there was the best lounge. That overlooked the part of the garden where there were steps down. It was just beautiful. Then you went through into what we called the back kitchen, where the dumb waiter was and I presume that's where they did all the catering, when there was a function on and then you went back out into the hall.

The library was originally in the building. It was on the first floor and I think it was initially the library from the hall from when it was used as a home. There was a sign on the door that said 'Library'. A lot of the rooms were labelled. It was purpose built, because they were proper shelves and they looked as old as the panelling. It was near the bit we used to call 'the hole in the floor' with the landing. That was the public library before they built the one in the grounds, which broke my heart, because they cut down all my trees. In the stables the groundsmen used to keep their lawnmowers and wheelbarrows. In front of the bowling green there was the putting green.

Kate Kerry

Searching for Work

My father was a turner by trade. I remember mother saying that on occasions he was up during the night to walk [from Droylsden] to places like Bolton and the other side of Manchester, when he heard that there were jobs available, which was a terrific distance,

Kate Kerry's mother, Constance (Connie) Bradshaw on the occasion of her marriage to Graham Newton in 1950. With her is her father, Frank, and on the left Vera and Roy Wilson, the best man, at Ryecroft Hall, where Kate's grandparents were the caretakers.

when you think about it these days. Of course, even walking to Bolton, he wasn't always lucky to be given a job, when he got there, because there probably would be one or two hundred other people waiting as well.

Fred Lord

Out Of Work in the Twenties

When the engineers were on strike, I can remember it now seeing my father with a collecting box outside the Stamford cinema. He wasn't collecting for himself: they collected because they didn't get any wages.

Fred Clark

63

CHAPTER 4
Farming

George Walker aged four in 1937 outside the old shippon (cowshed) in the farmyard at Jaum Farm in Littlemoss, where his family farmed. Later they moved to King's Road Farm by the reservoirs in Audenshaw, where George farmed until his retirement.

Around Littlemoss

As you go deeper into Littlemoss, you come to the bend where the old Co-operative Society building used to be and on that corner is a farm called Cinderland Hall, where the Cook family still live. Joe Cook was one of the members of my class at school. It was a mixed farm: I don't recall any milk rounds.

My school friends in the '30s and '40s were Reg and Jean Whitehead; they were twins from Jaum Fields Farm. John and Fred Barker lived in the house on Plantation Lane. John and Joseph Ollerenshaw, who still occupy Buckley Hill Farm on Cross Lane, were also my friends and Tony and Margaret Littlewood, who lived at Blake Rake cottage, also on Back Lane. Then

From left to right, Bob, Charly Foly, Sammy Jones and Jack Walker by the gate to the yard at Jaum Farm, where Jack and George's father farmed, in 1935.

there was Alan Thomas from Morningside. When you came from Daisy Nook along Back Lane, you turned left at the crossroads up Plantation Lane to go up to Hope Fold, where the Rothwells used to live. He was a woodcutter, who lived here with his wife and three boys. There was Charlie the eldest, Jimmy and little Arthur. Over the railway was Moss Bank Farm, which a man by the name of Hickey Hough lived in. When I was a lad, a Mr Jones was the farmer at Crowhill. Lower Crowhill was further across again at Littlemoss and was occupied by the Walton family. Willow Bank Farm was occupied by a Mr Ivor Hadfield with his wife and daughter, Mary. Mr Hadfield used to breed very good collie dogs.

George Walker

Buckley Hill Farm

My grandma's uncle, Matthew Day, married a widow here, called Mrs Greenwood, in the 1870s, when the farm was owned by Stamford Estates and they would just be tenants. My grandparents bought the farm eventually. I think we had eighty-four acres at maximum. We used to keep about sixty cows and quite a lot of hens. During and before the war, they used to produce the milk here and retail it in Ashton. The farmhouse used to have inglenooks, seats in the alcoves round the fire. One or two cubby holes are still original; there's an oak cupboard in the chimney breast for salt to keep dry or to put tea in. They did use to have fireplaces in the bedrooms upstairs. The attic is still roughly the same with beams similar to the long barn, a bit twisting and turning. There's an oak staircase and a lot of the original, oak doors. In the bedrooms and other rooms, about fifty to sixty years ago, somebody modernising it boxed the beams in. They all look nice and square. In old houses like this you seem to go from one room to another. Even some of the bedrooms, you've got to walk through one bedroom to get to the other one. All the windows in the attic and one or two others round the other side and round the back were bricked up in the reign of William III, when they started charging tax on light, the window tax. We were clearing the attic out and we found a coin dating back to 1675, Charles II. Somebody up there dropped that in about 1680. It just puts it in perspective. I've heard it said Oliver Cromwell stopped here overnight but we've nothing to prove it.

Joe Ollerenshaw

Jaum Farm

I was born at Jaum Farm in 1933 at the end of Back Lane and its neighbouring farm is Jaum Fields Farm, which in those days was occupied by the Jim Whitehead family. Jaum Farm had some forty odd acres of land. My father, George Walker, rented this from the Stamford Estates. It was a farm consisting mainly of peat and moss land, which in places was very difficult to cultivate, because of its boggy nature. There were fields around the farm property, which were reasonably solid to work on but nearer to the railway line, which intercepted the farmland, the ground there in places was somewhat dangerous. We had two fields at the top of Back Lane, which was facing the new council houses, which ran along the main Lumb Lane. In fact, as a boy, when we used to plough, I would follow behind and

The milk float of the Walker family outside their home at Jaum Farm in Littlemoss, in the early 1930s. On the left is Vera, George and Jack's sister, holding the silver trophy won at Mottram Show for the Best Dairy Breed Champion.

The farm workers' cottages at World's End Farm on Benny Lane in 1967. The farm buildings were demolished in 1987 to make way for a housing development.

there were always lots and lots of clay pipes there. When we first moved to Jaum Farm, my father was the first farmer in that area to grow corn on that particular field and he used to make the stooks with the hoods on the top, so that they were all in rows. When they were collected, then we used to make a corn rick at the farm itself.

George Walker

Along Benny Lane

George Dale, who used to be on Droylsden Council, used to live at World's End Farm. I can remember going down there to get wool off Mrs Dale, when we were knitting during the war [for the Services]. In more recent times the farm belonged to two brothers called Walker. They kept pigs and hens. At one time they had an egg-packing place and we used to go down and get eggs now and again. Inside there were tiny rooms with low ceilings. Benny Lane Farm was a little farm,

halfway down. It was more like a smallholding. All the land on Benny Lane was sold for building.

Jeanne Margerison

Milking and Haymaking

My family, George and Emma Nixon (*née* Sanderson), came [to Droylsden] when they got married in 1904 and my father had been working on one of the farms down Greenside Lane, not the 'Pig on the Wall' but one further down. They lived at No. 13, Oldham Street. There was a farm there just past the row of houses, called Duffy's Farm.

Dodd's Farm on Sandy Lane had two cottages attached to it. That was the most popular place for the children in the area to go and play. George Dodd used to come out regularly and say 'Clear off!' They did have cows. I used to go with a jug to get some milk occasionally. There was a dairy at the side of the house. It was just a bare, square

Benny Lane, Droylsden, near the gateway to Benny Lane Farm, in 1984.

room with a cooler with water running down, that they poured the milk into and into a churn. There was no pasteurisation. The milk used to taste queer sometimes, like turnips. It depended what the cows had been eating. There was also a big haystack with a roof on. They used to come out and cut the hay every year and we all used to come out, throw it about and get in the way generally. Then we used to play on the haystack. I remember a ladder fell on my nose on one occasion, a big farm ladder. I finished up at Ancoat's Hospital, having someone looking up my nose to see what had happened. The farmhouse was all pulled down, when these houses were built.

Jeanne Margerison

Around Shepley

The farm that we had was just at the end of Haughton Road. There was an iron foundry and a chemical works before they built those houses, just a bit further down, and this big farmhouse, called Kilshaw Farm. They took it down to put the council houses up. The people that lived there before us were called Cheetham. It belonged to a farm called Porritt's, that farm down the bottom of Shepley Road [Shepley Hall]. Porritt used to own it for years and years. A very big house it was. He went away and Phillip's took it over.

Ada Hammond

Shepley Hall Farm

In 1910 there were granddad and grandma, William Alderson and Cordelia Phillips, here. Eventually in 1968, when my grandma died, she left my father Shepley Hall Farm. The older part of the foundations are of sandstone and the barns are hand-made brick, possibly 1770-

Dodd's Farm on Sandy Lane, Droylsden, in the 1960s. The farmhouse on the right adjoins a barn, which is attached to the three farm workers' cottages on the left.

1780. Shepley Hall farmhouse was built later, about 1860. I know because the barn here, some of those vents go down the side, which actually open up into the house but this house wall goes straight against it.

Ben Phillips

Watch Out!

I was frightened to death of those cows. They used to take them all across Denton Road to the fields on the left-hand side of the road, as Clayton's was on the right-hand side. When we were waiting for the tram to come and these cows came, I used to hide in the little gardens in front of the houses and my mother was a farmer's daughter!

Joan Jebb

Ben Phillips at the door to his farmhouse at Shepley Hall Farm in 2000, just prior to demolition. Ben is holding a picture of his farm showing the layout of the barns and farmyard.

Saxon Fold Farm

The farm was built about 1400, I think, and the new part 1719. There were big, thick walls, a nice big inglenook and a great big iron fireplace. You could keep books and treasures on top of the beam that went across. I was big enough to have a rocking chair and I used to sit there with my granddad. He used to read to me as it went dark and across the fields you could see the lights of the brickyard. Then my uncle would go out and bring the cows in and he knew every one by name: he was that type of person.

Originally the farm went right the way through to Stamford Road and then they started to build; Alan Dean built the houses on that estate and of course the farm went smaller. Mainly I remember the main field, the hay field, was up to the railway on this side. Then there was another meadow facing us, going up towards the brickworks. There were allotments all round the side. They decided that they would like more clay and so they pulled the farm down in 1959.

It was a nice, comfortable building. We had a gas light in one room: it was all oil lamps and candles. We had a boiler for boiling the clothes in a corner of the kitchen but we had to carry any hot water through from the living room. So, on very cold winter nights, I'm afraid we used to bring a great big bowl into the living room. The beam coming in at the front door was very low and people, who didn't know, and

The pond on the farm land of Clayton's Farm behind Denton Road, Audenshaw, in 1929. Bessie Watt and her elder sister Mary stand by the pond behind their home and in the background is Kilshaw Lane, now known as St Anne's Road.

some people that did know, really cracked their head, if they forgot to duck down. Above it were gun racks; we never had guns on them but they were there. We went through from the living room to a partition and then to a larder and grandma had orange boxes made into cupboards in there and a frill curtain across them. Then you went down a step and into the actual kitchen. Outside there was the toilet. The night soil men used to come. It was a flat top with just a hole in it.

We went through from the living room, through the corridor and towards the stairs and there was a door down the side of the stairs that went underneath the house and was called a water cellar. I never went down. There were two rooms, one each side of the front door. We used one of them as an office. The other one was the front room and my grandma had things like silver covered in glass cases on the sideboard.

Upstairs there were just three rooms, of course no bathroom. One room was enormous. It had two double beds in it, great big chests of drawers, a great big wardrobe and you could still have had a dance in the middle of it. Then there was the main, my grandma's bedroom, which had a window on either side and a lovely little fireplace, which was great, because when you were ill you got a coal fire. At the back there was the room that I had and I liked this one particularly, because you could go out of the window. The sloping roof of the coalhouse took you down into the garden. It was a rambling garden. We used to grow dahlias and beautiful raspberries we had. The front door we never used: we always used the one out of the farmyard. There was a cottage next door, where the Kettlestrings lived.

Betty Slater

On the left Thomas Henry Gregory stands next to his son, James Robert Gregory, in front of the stone bridge coming from Groby Road, in their fields at Saxon Farm in Audenshaw in the 1930s. Betty Slater is the granddaughter of Thomas and daughter of James.

Along Stamford Road

I used to go to Reece's farm Sundays sometimes. There was my uncle Jim [Reece], my father's brother, and my auntie, Mary Ann. Of course there were quite a few sisters that used to play with us. Bob, one of the sons, was blind. He went to Henshaw School in Manchester. There were Maude, Mary and Minnie. The farm was just over the bridge on Stamford Road, as you went from the main road at Audenshaw, on the right

The Reece family outside their farmhouse on Stamford Road in the early 1900s. The family consisted of Leah, Minnie, Maude, May and Bob with their mother Mary Ann, father Jim and grandmother Reece. Their niece Mabel used to visit as a child.

hand side there. I think there's houses built there now. It was set back; you went down steps to get to it but it wasn't very far from the main road.

Mabel Lawson

Boothcote Farm

I've lived there [Boothcote Farm] about fifty-three years. It was Higginbottom that owned it before. It belonged to the seventh Earl of Stamford and Warrington. We lived in it so many years before we bought it. I was twenty when we went to the farm. I am seventy-five now. The time's gone! We started keeping cows, a horse or two, hens, chickens and geese. My father had milk rounds. There was a big dairy, a shippon and a big hay thing at

the side. The front door of the house was at the side opposite the steps and you went round to the garden to that porch. There was a wash house at side. There was one big barn.

Ada Hammond

Coming for the Milk

There was Ellis' farm just over where Woodbridge [Avenue] is at the back of the fields. It was a dairy and when I was a little girl, if you wanted milk, you used to go there to get a pint of milk with a jug. I think somebody bought the land to build on and from the farm they came to live here [Woodbridge].

Florence Dyson

High Ash near Red Hall

It had a lovely dairy, very, very cool, and great grandma used to do butter in there and cheeses: there was usually a cheese under the table in the parlour. They had the cows and I can remember going into the shippon and having milk straight from the cow, warm milk. They had pigs too and hens. Dad was one of six but my granddad was one of ten, so there were quite a lot of great aunts and uncles always bobbing in and out. The farm was eventually split into two dwellings so that Uncle Charlie could live in the front half and grandma and granddad lived in the back in the best parlour and they shared the kitchen. We never went in the front door: we always went round the back to a side door. The kitchen had a flag floor with a staircase going off with a door on the staircase and there was always a big range with a fire in it. Whenever you opened the back door all the cats came round: there were kittens all the time, but it kept the mice down. There were horses in the field and a pond at the far end where the flats are now at the bottom, fed by a natural spring. They used the reservoir embankment and the home field, which is where Trafalgar Estate is now. That big house there was a girls' home and we used to call it the 'home field'. So we'd hay make down there and that came right back to Lumb Lane, behind Noblett's. The memorial gardens, we called it the 'three corner field' because, if you look at it, it's a three corner. He farmed all down here, at the bottom of Spring Bank, before all these houses were built.

Dorothy Clinton

Cornhill Lane and King's Road

There is Debdale Farm, which has now been developed into private properties. Old Mr Goddard he occupied and farmed it for a good many years: he was still farming when we moved here in 1943. They had three daughters, Anice, Winnie and Dorothy. Then there was Tom, the only son, and he lived at Lodge Farm. I think old Mr Goddard lived at Lodge Farm originally, until he retired and moved to Debdale.

Lodge Farm is further up the lane. The front corner is obviously quite modern but when you go within the house, it's very,

Alec Campbell, Christine Grimshaw's father, with 'Dolly' on Sandringham Avenue, Audenshaw, in July 1960. The farm land belonged to Boothcote farm with Trafalgar cricket pavilion in the far off field and beyond that the buildings of Planet Foundry and General Gas Appliances on Corporation Road.

very quaint in the middle section, which gives the impression that it is a house of some great age. This may reflect itself in the barn at the top of Cornhill Lane, which again has considerable age about it. It appears to me to be a building, which might have been used many years ago for the storage of corn, because of all the ventilation holes in the walls and the round hole at the apex of the building. There is a croft, which leads from the back of Lodge Farm straight up to the farmyard itself. I would have thought that this was really the barn at the top of the lane, belonging to Lodge Farm.

Prior to the reservoirs being built, King's Road was known as Dick Lane. Dick Lane Farm was situated just in the little path that leads onto the golf course there and I think

that led to the farm entrance. I've located Dick Lane Farm as being where the gateway is, approximately just to the right, on what would be now a golf course. There was a little crop of buildings at the bottom of that lane, which Fairfield golf club kept their tractors in and their greens-mowing equipment. The lane ended just below the farm.

King's Road Farm must have been built about 1890. The barn is not a typical Lancashire farm building: it's very long, two hundred and seventy feet long. It has a first storey to it, a loft for storing hay, and the windows are quite large. Someone suggested to me it was a dormitory for the navvies [building the canal] and I think it was purpose built. King's Road Farm used to consist of something like seventy acres of

The Worthington family outside No. 228 Audenshaw Road, High Ash Farm, in 1899. Alfred Senior, together with his wife Anne, poses with his ten children. Dorothy Clinton is the daughter of Bertram Worthington and is the great granddaughter of Alfred and Anne.

King's Road Farm on King's Road, Audenshaw in the early 1990s. On the left is the farmhouse with the long barn to the right and the banking of the reservoir behind it.

land. My father took over this tenanted farm from the Bradleys in 1943, when I was just ten years of age. My father had two men and Jack, my brother. By 1956, there were just myself, Jack and my father. The horses had dwindled from five down to two and those were kept mainly for the milk round but able to do a bit of land work. Jack and I, our farming partnership continued up until 1959, steadily progressing, and then we were informed that some fifty acres of the land at King's Road were to be taken from the farm for the use of the golf course. Jack moved to Woodley and I stayed here. I keep beef cattle here now. I buy them in as young calves and rear them on and then sell them. I'm a bottled milk buyer and I keep poultry. I've got only twenty-two acres and they are all embankments [of the reservoirs] apart from the flat land above it and the farm buildings. This area is all part of a planned development [1991].

George Walker

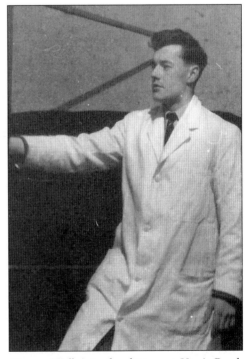

George Walker in the shippon at King's Road Farm in the early 1950s, stock judging dairy cows. The farm was demolished to make way for housing and industrial development.

CHAPTER 5
Shopping and Deliveries

Jack Walker returning with 'Bobby' to King's Road Farm from his milk round in the 1960s. Jack originally farmed here with his father and then his brother George, but eventually moved out to Woodley, leaving George at King's Road.

Delivering Milk

We had three separate milk rounds in the '40s and, when I left school, I was put to manage and run one of them in the area around Roker Park, Aldwyn Park and Audenshaw Road. The delivery vehicles then were horse-drawn, although we did have a small delivery van as well. We would go by horse and milk float to the level

crossing by Moss Side Farm, cross the railway line and go along Ashton Moss Lane to the main crossroad in the middle of Ashton Moss. Now this was a very wide lane, basically a cinder track with very deep ditches or dykes on each side. Eventually we would go onto Earl Street in Ashton where the milk round would begin, all around that part of Ashton right up to Guide Bridge. Another milk round, done with a small van,

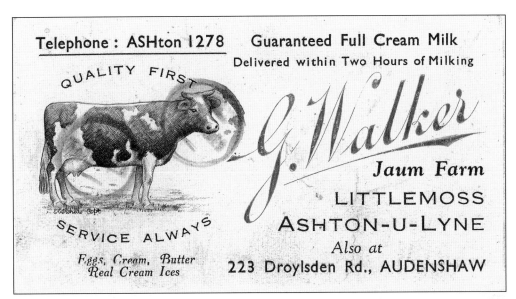

The business card of George Walker's father, when he farmed at Jaum Farm on Littlemoss in the 1930s, until he moved to King's Road Farm in 1943.

was created by my two sisters, Vera and Joyce. They went all around the Hurst area, as far as the Broadoak, during the 1930s and 1940s.

In the winter and in the spring you could smell the tangy odour of the celery in the morning frost, which is a lovely smell and never to be forgotten. Sometimes, if we met the Ollerenshaws coming across the Moss on their way home, my dad would give our horse his head, a free rein, and a silent test of the best horse would ensue. If you felt cold crossing the Moss in winter on the milk float, you would be told to step off the back step, hang onto the rear handle, while the cart was going, run like mad 'til you were breathless and step on again. That really warmed you up!

The milk in those days was placed in ten gallon churns. When you arrived on the streets, Dad would fill small cans and you would go to the appropriate doorstep and pour your can into the awaiting jug on the step, first removing the muslin cover or saucer from the jug. There had to be no careless spilling on the step. That was the golden rule, for most of the steps were donkey stoned, either cream colour or brown, and the women were most fastidious about their front doorsteps. There was one particular customer, who always gave me the jitters. She would stand waiting at the door and you got her sharp tongue, if you spilled even a drop.

George Walker

Serve Me First

George [Walker] came with the milk. He reminded me very much of my brother that had been killed in the war and I always had a soft spot for George. The trouble was I was always the last to be served and then he would say 'I'm going back now, finished'. So

The dairy of the Walker family at the corner of Assheton Avenue on the right and Manchester Road, Audenshaw, around 1931. On the left stands Joyce with her mother Annie (née Bagshaw). The two daughters, Vera and Joyce, ran the newly built shop from 1931.

I asked him one day if he would mind changing his rota and coming and serving me first. He said, 'I'm very sorry Mrs Conneely but the horse won't go that way: it knows its way round and it won't go any other way!'

Frances Conneely

Rely on the Horse

The horses knew where they were going along Garden Street. The man would just stop and get his milk and deliver it and the horse moved on to the next house. There was one house opposite. It always used to

stop there, because they had a crust for it – horse sense!

Bill Pollitt

At the Dairy

At No. 223, Droylsden Road, on the corner of Assheton Avenue, my two sisters, through the war years, used to open the shop up for half the day and eventually they opened it full-time, when they stopped doing the milk round. Now one of my sisters, Vera, was very talented at window dressing and at different times of the year to mark certain events, like Christmas time and Easter time, she would make special exhibitions in the window. She really was very talented but she didn't appreciate how good she was at such things.

George Walker

Home Delivery

In the early 1900s mother was wakened by the hoof beats of the horse pulling the newspaper cart at five in the morning. Fruit and green groceries were brought round on Fridays on a cart driven by Ted Whitehead. Mrs Mills pushed a heavy, iron-wheeled cart from Hanover Street, near Guide Bridge, to sell fish and rabbits. She had a small table top on the cart and she cleaned and filleted the fish, and skinned and cut up the rabbits out in the street. Her husband 'Fish Jimmy' plied the same trade in Ashton using a horse and cart. Fresh herrings were seven for 3d,

cod was 2 ½ d for a lb and white salmon (hake) was 5d a lb. Coal was 6d a bag.

Arthur Bantoft

Fish to the Door

On Guide Lane, on the corner of Providence Street, my mother and father had a fish shop and my father ran a fish round, originally by horse and cart. Then he went into a motorbike and sidecar. During the week the sidecar was taken off and a box was put on with the fish in and the scales and then, come weekend, we used to put the sidecar back on. He advanced from that to a three-wheeler van and eventually, just after the war, he bought a Morris Eight car, had the passenger seat removed and the box put in there. So he used that as a van. The box came out again at weekends. We used to go for a ride in the car at weekends. It didn't always smell good!

Robert (Bob) Slater standing by his motorbike and sidecar, from which he ran a mobile fishmongery business, while his wife ran a fresh fish shop on Guide Lane, in the 1920s.

Bob Slater serving a customer with fish from his trailer attached to his car on Stamford Road in 1959.

An advertisment for the coal merchants, Alan and Fred Gregory of Saxon Farm on Stelfox Lane, Audenshaw, in 1949. The business was bought by Bill Pollitt, who was married to Brenda Gregory.

Eventually [late 1940s] he got a better car, a new Ford Prefect. He had his trailer on the back and so the car smelt a lot better! My mother had the shop: she sold just fish and eggs. In the house in Paradise Street, we had a cellar, which was another reason we moved there, because my father could keep his cold box down there for the fish and at Christmas time it was full of chickens and turkeys and what have you. It was cool of course.

Harry Slater

Delivering Coal

At the top [of Saxon Farm yard] my uncle had a part there; he had a green grocery round in Audenshaw and he used to run his business from there and my father used it to garage his coal lorry. After the war, Alan and Fred [Gregory] went into the coal business together and it's not long since they finished. My father was a coal merchant in Audenshaw [James Robert Gregory] and Uncle Milton was a coal merchant in Fallowfield.

Betty Slater

Just Left the Money on the Table

I took J.R. Gregory's coal business over. Brenda's father died and her son and uncle ran the business for Brenda's mother. Eventually the business was up for sale: I bought it and ran it until the advent of smokeless zones, which saw the business off. I was based at Audenshaw on Hay Street off Guide Lane, opposite Manor Street. There were no houses on it, just a small factory and this big yard that I had. The coal round was still in the days when you didn't have to lock your doors. People would know I was coming and leave money under the mat or on the kitchen table. It was all coal, when I took the business over [1970s]. Gradually with the advent of smokeless zones, people were turning to gas or to smokeless solid fuel, which really complicated the matter, because you had so much to choose from. We used to say, 'Mrs So and So's gassed herself'. Gradually the business just went down and down and down. The coal came by rail to Guide Bridge Station from Yorkshire. Quite a lot of smokeless fuel came by road or we used to go to the gas works for it in Denton. There were dozens of coal merchants and all kept busy. Gradually I took on the rounds of different people and that lasted for quite a while. The business closed in the '70s.

Bill Pollitt

Henry Mellor's Coal Yard

There was a coal merchant's, Henry Mellor's coal yard, where Brother's and the bank is. You went in off Guide Lane through an archway into the coal yard at the back. He had stacks of coal there and he used to have his wagons coming in, and then he had a taxi service. He was a carrier.

Betty Slater

Working in the Stables

In the 1920s my father was working, by the time I was born, at Droylsden Co-op. He delivered coal with a horse and cart. Also, of course, there were stables for the horses and this is how he got his job, because he could look after the horses. The stables were on Dunkirk Street.

Jeanne Margerison

Moss Celery!

On Sunday mornings many men with handcarts would leave the Moss, via Manchester Road, all loaded with a variety of vegetables and celery to tour the nearby streets, as far away as Openshaw. 'Celery, Moss celery' was then the cry, when they reached the customers and by one o'clock you would see them all coming back, having completely sold up. There was a firm in Lower Openshaw, that used to hire out a wooden box with long handles to it and its wheels were usually two mangle wheels. These men would go round calling 'Rag! Bone!' usually collecting old clothes and woollens, and then return to the firm, who then in turn would pay them for the rags and woollens that they brought in. It was 2s 6d to hire the box on wheels for the day.

George Walker

Ice Cream

I always thought that because H. Traynor's wife was Italian, that's why his ice cream was so sought after. He used to go out with his ice cream cart and sell it. During the war there were less ice cream parlours anyway. Just after the war, when things began to get better, it used to go round, 'Traynor's, they've got some ice cream!' and people would get over to Traynor's before he'd sold it all. He was at No. 92, Audenshaw Road, just up from Guide Bridge on the right hand side, near Hanover Street, near the Church Inn.

Bill Pollitt

Near Red Hall

There were a few local shops in the early 1900s. The post office was at No. 1, Chapel Street (later Edward Street) and was run by the Slack family. They also sold treacle and a variety of medicines, which were measured out into your own bottle. They later moved to Audenshaw Road, on the corner of Ash Street, nearest to Manchester. Next to the school was Taylor's shop. Mrs Taylor boiled

George Nixon, father of Jeanne Margerison, with his horse at the Co-op stables on Dunkirk Street, Droylsden, in the 1940s. George worked as a coalman for the Co-op.

her own ham and sold all manner of foods: corned beef, yeast (balm) and tripe on a Friday.

Arthur Bantoft

Couldn't Drag Ourselves Away

On winter evenings, in the 1930s, we, who played out after tea, would congregate around the lighted shop window. There we played our games in the gaslight. Dark curtains hung down, separating the window space from the shop. Now and again, these would part swiftly as the elderly shopkeeper dived through to take a handful of plush nuggets or coconut chips from the open boxes. These she would weigh on the polished brass scale and tip into a three cornered bag, torn swiftly from a thick pile, threaded on string and hanging from a nail. Just before Christmas time we could hardly bear to leave that window. It was filled with iced Christmas cakes, each with its bright frill and topped with a snowman or a tiny figure on a sledge. Each cake had a pencilled price ticket and the biggest and best of all cost 5s. That seemed a princely sum for a cake with both a robin and Father Christmas on top. On pressing the latch the bell above the door gave a single sharp note. Then the warm and comforting smell of baking would envelop you. There, for only 1d, you could buy a raspberry bun or a jam puff, oozing jam at the edges. Very special cream buns cost only one ha'penny more, whilst large fruit pies, baked on a dinner plate, could be had for 8d or a half pie for 4d or a single piece for a 1d. Oh, but the meat pies! Real big ones with a raised top, full of lean meat and piping hot, thin gravy and all for 3d. Miss Annie, stiff and severe, did the

baking and only rarely came into view. Miss Ellen, her sister, reigned behind the counter, sitting upon a high stool with the seat upholstered in red plush and wearing, winter and summer, a hat!

Lena Slack

The Most Amazing Pies

In the 1940s there was a house that was quite a long frontage: that was a chip shop and green grocer's shop, Mr Dawson's. He had a lot of shops. On the very corner was the cake shop, which sold wonderful pies, the house that's on the corner with the big bay windows. That was the pie shop and then they moved down towards near the Blue Pig next to Noblett's. That's closed but, when I first came to Audenshaw, it was an old lady's called Essie Taylor's sweet shop. When they opened it as a decorator's shop, before it was a pie shop, they still used the same counter and the same little drawers for putting stuff in, and the same shelves. It's gone now and the post office has gone.

Dorothy Clinton

Corner Shops

My mother had a shop, Pearson's. It was No. 1, right on the corner of Moorside Street and there were lots and lots of terraced houses in streets around there, presumably built at one time for the mill workers. There was a bit of a tick system: sometimes people didn't pay till Friday. There were no bad debts as far as I remember: everybody would pay up in the end. You could actually buy two woodbines; you didn't have to buy a packet. Do you remember the little paper woodbine packets? Of course, during the war tobacco was much more difficult because it was all under the counter stuff then. We were rationed but not officially. The shop was open in the evening until seven or eight. It wasn't selling alcohol; the outdoor [outdoor beer licence] was Eastward's which was across the way. They had much longer hours: it was a bigger shop.

John Pearson

Limited Shopping

Audenshaw Road was very poor for shopping. When I came here at first in the 1940s, there was the butcher's, grocer's, hairdresser's and newsagent's. The grocer's is now closed, the butcher's is a fish and chip, then there's the newsagent's and the hairdresser's is closed.

Margaret Slater

Shopping On the Corner

In the 1960s I shopped at the local shops on the corner [Assheton Avenue]. There was Walker's who had the grocery shop, the dairy on the corner and a haberdashery. There was a chemist, the butcher, the greengrocer of course and a very nice confectioner, although I always did my own, but when I was stuck I used to go there. There were, I would say, three grocers on this corner. Of course, with my husband coming home to lunch every day and the

Audenshaw Road, running east towards Guide Bridge, in the early 1900s. On the right is the Hanging Gate Inn and on the left Dennell's general store. On the distant bend stand the cottages by Groby Road, built for railway employees.

children coming home for school dinners made it that I had to shop on the corner or else each Tuesday one of the neighbours and I used to push our prams to Ashton. But we had to be back for children out of school or husbands out of work.

Frances Conneely

Quarp

As a child in the 1920s everyone referred to the 'Quarp' and I grew up wondering what was meant by 'Quarp' milk and 'Quarp' coal. I sometimes went to the Co-op shop just up the road and I loved it. The male assistants wore white cotton jackets and long, white aprons down to their feet. They called me 'Dolly' and I had quite a crush on one, who having made a neat brown paper parcel of the sugar, tea and butter, would tie it securely with string and then break the string by a swift sideways tug. The Co-op had a stand on the counter with three plate glass shelves, on which were displayed the cakes and pastries and among them triangular shaped sponge cakes with a thick layer of cream, bearing a ticket which said 9d. My greatest desire was that some day my mother would let me bring one of these for our weekend tea but she never did.

Lena Slack

The Co-op

At the end here there was a Co-op and the paper shop, where they made them into flats. Then there was a Co-op too at the top of Sidmouth Street here, where Californian Wines is. My friend Daisy used to leave a list

DROYLSDEN CO-OPERATIVE SOCIETY LIMITED

	Membership	Sales
1934	10,159	£355,930
1935	10,706	£385,664
1936	11,497	£409,222
1937	12,202	£443,149

It's worth while to Shop at the CO-OP.

DROYLSDEN CO-OPERATIVE SOCIETY LIMITED

An advertisement of 1938 for the Droylsden Co-operative Society, whose large store still dominates the crossroads at the corner of Market Street and Manchester Road in Droylsden town centre. Audenshaw was served by the Ashton Co-operative Society.

in the morning on the way to work and then pick it up on the way back. It had a bacon slicer and coffee grinders. We didn't have the pool cards here for the money like they did in Openshaw and Droylsden.

Dorothy Clinton

Guide Lane Co-ops

Then there was Kilshaw Lane and the road came round and there was the Co-op. Everyone went to the Co-op: there was the Divi. There was the Co-op Drapery and then the Co-op Grocery. In the 1930s, I

Advertisements of 1924 for various shops along Guide Lane, Audenshaw, which was lined with shops of all kinds, before demolition in the 1970s to realign the road and junction at the Pack Horse Inn.

used to drop a little red notebook off on a Tuesday morning, and push it through the letterbox if they hadn't opened. By the afternoon they would have delivered the order, all wrapped up in beautiful, brown paper parcel, strung up and delivered on a horse and cart. Then you used to go in and pay and you used to go up the stairs into the big room to draw your Divi.

Bessie Watt

The Co-ops Near Red Hall

On the corner, the Ashton Co-op had a shop, the living quarters upstairs being reached from a door and stairs on Ash Street.

Arthur Bantoft

Cutting the Butter

The Co-op was quite a big shop. It was an old shop with massive counters and they used to cut the butter and pat it and cut it in pieces for you. There was the general store; next to it was the butcher's. It was on the part of Guide Lane that used to come from the Stamford, Sun Inn, stretch; over the Co-op was Ford's Dancing Academy.

Bill Pollitt

Big Counters

There were two Co-ops, one at top and one opposite facing Bridge Street: that was a big Co-op opposite Bridge Street. You went in and there were great big counters all the way around. There was a separate butchers.

Betty and Harry Slater

Shopping along Guide Lane

We went shopping in Hooley Hill. It was a real good shopping centre, Guide Lane: everything that you could mention and they were good shops – Hampson's outfitter's, Jackson's grocer's, Jones' high class fruiterer's, Miss Jones' milliner's, and the Co-op.

Dale Street went up the side of the Co-op. It sold everything, although *we* didn't go to the Co-op.

Ruth Rogerson

He Was a Character

The family bought their meat from Grundy's, at the corner of Shepley Road, run by the father and two sons. One son, Jack, came round on a Friday evening to take orders. He was a character! He would say, 'We have beef, mutton, lamb, veal, pork, corned beef and pickled tongue. Splendid meat and a lovely butcher!' Jack was the salesman and the other brother, Arthur, was the buyer. He went to market early in the morning to buy cattle. Another brother had his own butcher's shop in Droylsden.

Arthur Bantoft

Shopping Every Day

Guide Lane was the main street in what was known as Hooley Hill. This main street had more shops than I could count, shops that sold everything we could possibly want, food, meat, dresses, shoes, hats, furniture, pianos, post office, coal yard and grocery. So we could buy anything we needed or could afford. We had no way of keeping food fresh, so we bought fresh food every day in small quantities. On New Year's Day gangs of children used to go into the shops and wish the owner a Happy New Year, and if we were lucky we would be given an orange, but, as I remember, these were very small and very sour.

Vera Worth

The Different Shops

Right opposite the smithy there was a butcher's called Robinson's. That was right next to the church. He used to do his own killing. His brother, Ted, was the big butcher: I think he did the killing and Arthur only had the selling in the shop. It closed when all the shops and everything went on Guide Lane. Up to the new road coming, Guide Lane was shops all the way down: a beautiful hat shop, a big, bird and animal feed shop just where the pub is next door to the precinct and a herbalist. Connie and Alf had a high-class gents' outfitter's. There was a music and a millinery shop. Across the corner was a chip shop. Coming back onto Bridge Street side, there was an off-licence. Coming up there was a belting bread shop that did hot muffins. There was a butcher's, bread shop, sweets/tobacconist's and McVee's grocer's shop, where they used to deliver, on the corner opposite, where Guide Lane church is, where the post office is. He used to deliver all round the area. He had a delivery boy system. Then McAvoy's shop was on the bend: I used to go and make orders up there for him. As a boy I used to bag sugar. I used to pat the butter into blocks.

Harry Slater

Proper Chocolates

Further along Guide Lane there was a beautiful embroidery shop and a sweet shop on the corner. Then another bread shop down the side. Opposite the Pack Horse was quite a classy sweet shop. They had real chocolates. Dick Bowen had a little hut on Stamford Road. He sold sweets at this end

where the council houses are. We used to get sweets going on the way to Poplar Street to school. Jebb's was on the corner of St Anne's Road. On the other corner was Brindley's greengrocer's. Then on the other corner was the butcher's and Rose's lower down.

Harry and Betty Slater

Our Sweetshop

My first memories are going to visit my grandma – she'd taken over the shop in 1913 and it was on the corner of Stamford Road, opposite the Pack Horse there. When she passed away, my aunt took over and I used to help all the years then. When my aunt was ready to retire, she took over our house in Denton and we moved to the shop. We were in from 1953-1978 for twenty-six years. People knew me as I was growing up,

Derek Gregory stands with his sister Jean on Hazel Street, Audenshaw, in the 1930s. Behind them is the fencing round the fields of their grandparents' home, Saxon Farm, and on the far right is the sweetshop of Dick Bowen.

Jebb's sweetshop at the corner of Guide Lane on the left and Denton Road in 1977. The shop is decked out to celebrate the Jubilee of Queen Elizabeth II but the following year it was vacated by the Jebbs and demolished for road widening.

Joan Jebb's husband John serving in his sweetshop on Guide Lane in January 1964.

who I was serving, and it came that I was serving their children and then their grandchildren! You could get a whole quarter of sweets for 2d. They used to come in big blocks, thick lumps and you had to chop them up. My aunt had a sort of chopper on a piece of wood that opened and you chopped. She used to let us chop it up for her: you could weigh a quarter of a pound out. Everything was loose: no packaging. The same with tobacco: you had to weigh it. Across the road was Charlie Smith's and further down was the Sun Inn. As you walked along Guide Lane, the whole right hand side of Guide Lane was all shops; you didn't need to go out of the town for anything. There was grocers, sweetshop, photographers, furniture shop, lovely ladies' hatshops for Whitsuntide hats, pawnbroker,

bakers. That went on right to the bottom of Guide Lane. There were six pubs, I think, from the top near the Pack Horse to the corner, where the Sun Inn was – only about twenty-five yards. Eventually they did take the corner down in '78.

Joan Jebb

CHAPTER 6
During the Wars

Dorothy Clinton (née Worthington) stands second from the left with her cousin Roy Worthington on the left, while May Elwell steadies Susan Bridge on the right, around 1946. They are playing off Williamson Lane, Droylsden, on former farm land at the back of Droylsden Road, with air raid shelters in the background.

World War One

Moving Memories

We lived in Ancoats, Manchester. I had a big family and I had one brother who was a prisoner of war for three and a half years, and one brother was killed. My mother was always weeping when she got letters. My mother was so upset and distraught that my father got a house in Audenshaw near to her sister and brought us all up here to try to take my mother's mind off the tragedy. I was two years old; it was 1916.

After the war, my mother got a pension, 7s 2d a week and she had to go to the post office: I used to go with her. She used to give me this 2d to have a comic, 'Chip's Own'. Oh, it was the highlight of the week but, when I came home, my father used to take it and read it and we couldn't have it until he'd read it.

Vera Worth

Off To War

I went to Bridge Street School and they had a Young Men's class of forty odd. There were only about ten of them left behind and a lot of them never came back. My husband went through it but he was fortunate – he came back.

Ruth Rogerson

On Munitions

My mother used to talk about being 'on munitions' at Belle Vue. As my father was in France, she had to take my sister, then only a baby, to stay with relatives from Monday to Friday, and she had hated those years because she felt she was deprived of the joy in caring for her only child – a beautiful, dark curly haired, little girl. Then, too, the army pay was very small, and the rations only minimal, and my mother, along with countless others had a lean time of it in every way, working long shifts on war work, taking her child to a distant relative several miles away every Monday and going to fetch her on Friday, washing, cleaning, all to be done with none of the things we have today to make light of these jobs.

Lena Slack

Lena Slack's mother, Selina Johnson, in the garden of the Blue Pig public house on Audenshaw Road, around 1912. Selina came to Audenshaw from Openshaw to be a nursemaid at the Blue Pig and worked on munitions during the First World War.

Ryecroft Hall

My Mum, Phoebe, was one of those people, who helped out. Every street had one in those days – delivering babies, laying out people when they'd died and that kind of thing. She'd actually spent some time during the First World War working at Ryecroft Hall as a nursing auxiliary, helping to care for the wounded soldiers that came back from France. So she had some slight medical knowledge.

Fred Lord

An Explosion

About 1917, there was an explosion in Oxford Street [Guide Bridge]. I was working at Jones' at the time. I was up in the top room and I was on a little piece of wood to stand on to do my work. There was this hectic bang and I thought, 'That's a bomb'. It just sounded as though it had run right round the side of the building. Of course, we had a window in the roof. We pushed it open, climbed up and we could see the fire burning in a cotton mill. My husband's people lived opposite to it. Mrs Rogerson sent one of the girls up to our house out of the way. They sent everybody, who lived near the Moss, out of the way.

Ruth Rogerson

Armistice Day

My father went once a year on the nearest Sunday to November 11th for the Armistice Service. This he wouldn't have missed for anything. The ex-service men used to assemble in the square a few hundred yards from our Methodist chapel [Red Hall] for the evening service. There they would form up into columns and march the short distance down the road and into the church. This was a glorious occasion to me as a child. All the men were in their best suits, white stiff collars, and rows of medals gleaming on their brilliantly coloured ribbons. It was grand to see this solid phalanx of men filling the body of the church and to hear all those male voices sing, 'God, our help in ages past' and 'Abide with me'. There seemed to be a sea of

Lena Slack's elder sister Elizabeth (Betty) Johnson with her mother Selina and father Arthur, on the eve of his enlistment in the war in 1915. Sadly Elizabeth was to die of meningitis aged nineteen in 1933.

poppies, and the atmosphere was charged with a strange emotion.

At our school [Lumb Lane], Armistice Day was observed each year by a service in the hall. Some of the older scholars had lost their fathers in the war. The women teachers, all unmarried, wept and we believed that their sweethearts had been killed. One faded spinster wore a black dress and jet beads and looked as if life for her was over. At eleven o'clock, the hooters and blowers at the local factories sounded and we all closed our eyes at the melancholy sound. What a long time two minutes seemed, taken out of time and put by itself. The silence over, we coughed and shuffled. Then two scholars, whose fathers had been killed in battle, came out and hung a poppy wreath beneath a picture of a kneeling figure in armour.

The reading of the Roll of Honour came next, scholars of our school who had served in the war. I waited breathlessly as the headmaster read out the A's, the L's and on to the J's – my father's name and those of his three brothers. I was bursting with pride. And now, in softer tones, were read the names of those 'who made the supreme sacrifice' and included were my two uncles whom I had never seen.

Lena Slack

World War Two

A Child's View

I remember being at home on the day that war was declared with the radio on; everybody sat round waiting to hear what

John Pearson aged about fourteen around 1943, standing with his parents outside his home in Droylsden. He came to Droylsden in 1937, when he was seven, and lived on Moorside Crescent.

the decision would be and then a lot of sad faces, when they said we were at war with Germany. I thought to myself, 'I can't understand why they're looking so sad: it sounds very exciting to me!'

Fred Lord

At War

I remember war being declared; I would be nine. It was September the third. I remember sitting at the table and my mother was there and another lady. We listened to Chamberlain speaking and how upset my mother was because, obviously, she had lived through the First World War and knew what a terrible thing it was. When my father came home, I can remember him digging an air raid shelter in the garden, very early on. Then later on we had brick air raid shelters built in the garden.

John Pearson

Making Do

Of course, life changed dramatically then. All the lights went out. I remember the first time that the lights went out, a proper blackout with all the curtains closed and no light from any source really. It was unbelievable how dark it was. People were constantly walking into each other and into lamp-posts. The vehicle headlights were painted out with a half inch slit or a circular hole in the centre, just to let some light out, so that you could see them coming. People wore big sort of pin-on badges that were phosphorescent, so that you could see them coming in the dark.

Fred Lord

Never Wasted Paper

You just had to write on your exercise books [at Fairfield] and then turn them round and write the other way up in the spaces that you'd left, so there wasn't a space at all. There just weren't the books. In Maths, particularly, if you divided your page in half, you had to do two columns of sums. When you'd finished, you'd turn it round and filled

in the other gaps. If there were still gaps, you had to go back. You used every bit of paper: I don't like wasting paper now.

Margaret Walker

Bone Pie

At our shop the butter came in a lump and it all had to be cut up. Of course, you cut microscopic amounts of butter. I remember one lady came in and she had her ration on a slice of bread and she said, 'I had one good slice!' The meals were a bit odd. I remember once at Audenshaw Grammar School we had bone pie; I only had it once. It consisted of bones and pastry.

John Pearson

Never Seen a Banana

We were a big family and there was always somebody ready to help you. My mother-in-law used to say, 'We don't like eggs. Now we'll save eggs and give Eileen [Vera's baby] the eggs.' I didn't take sugar and so they could have my sugar. A lot of people did that. I had an elder sister, who was very like me. We used to go round every day, call at my mother's and have a cup of tea. This day she wasn't ready and I was in a hurry. As I passed the butcher's on Guide Lane, he called out and I said, 'Have the rabbits come?' 'No', he said, 'they're coming later'. In the meantime my sister had walked round and he thought it was me and he shouted, 'Your rabbit's come. Come on, quick!' So she came in and said, 'I've got a rabbit'. I could have hit her! We had half each. When the war was over, the first time the greengrocer called, I'd gone somewhere and Eileen came running after me. She said, 'Tom Slater's come, Mum, and he's left you some long, yellow things' – bananas! She'd never seen them before! We didn't come to any harm from it and there were always recipes coming on the wireless – Woolton Pie made out of vegetables. It was Lord Woolton who was in power.

Vera Worth

Business As Usual

I was eleven years old. Life carried on – we were used to hardship. Then rationing appeared – food, furniture, clothing. As we were already rationed by our economic situation, I think the main issue was food rationing. My mother worked wonders with our entitlement. Flour was brown and unrefined. I had the job of sieving the flour through an old lisle stocking, using the leg area. As the flour was shaken, the bran and the husks were left in the stocking. The white flour was shaken into bowls and we were treated to delicious, almost white, bread and muffins. At this time tins of blackcurrant puree were available from abroad. We used this on the bread – delicious!

Father went into the Forces in 1941 – extreme hard times for our mother. I know her stress was intense, although she never spoke of it. Caring for four children under these circumstances was dreadful. The children, myself included, made necklaces with chord and decorated the chord with seashells. We managed, with the help of

LANCASHIRE COUNTY COUNCIL
CIVIL DEFENCE DIVISION

DROYLSDEN URBAN DISTRICT COUNCIL

This is to certify that

Mrs. Lord has completed Care of the Homeless, Billeting and Evacuation training in the Welfare Section of the Droylsden. Division of the Civil Defence Corps and whilst remaining a full member of the Civil Defence Corps will henceforth normally be expected to attend only for refresher training and exercises.

Signed :

Chairman of the Council

Date 9th December, 1957.

A certificate achieved by Phoebe Lord as a member of the Civil Defence as preparation in post war uncertainty in 1957.

grandfather, to pierce the shell and sewed them to the chord. They sold well. Also we knitted dishcloths, embroidered and made tray cloths, table cloths, aprons and fancy doilies for standing treasured vases and bric-a-brac on, and knitted socks, gloves, scarves, and hats – all for the war effort. We raised money constantly for a Penny-a-Week fund for the Red Cross and St John's.

Dorothy Lord

Just a Laugh

We had to carry gas masks; I remember these cardboard gas masks and you had to practise putting them on. On the whole I think it was a great laugh, really. These

Rose Perfect (née Wilson) poses on the right with her sister Sally Ingham and brother Joseph Wilson, who returned safely from Dunkirk and later from Arnheim, in the 1940s.

cardboard boxes had a piece of string round your neck and you had to walk to school with them. We were all issued with them but it didn't seem for very long.

John Pearson

brought back with them (luxury indeed!) and also their tales of uniform clad, handsome, young men. Their uniforms were superior in cloth and fit to our soldiers'.

Dorothy Lord

The Americans Arrive

The Americans came to Burtonwood and attended dances at the Ritz and the Plaza in Manchester, armed with chocolates and silk stockings. I was told that many young ladies padded their bras with cotton wool and enjoyed jitterbugging and dancing with our American allies. When the ladies returned giggling, I saw my first pair of their gossamer silk stockings and I was overwhelmed that such leg coverings existed. I experienced some of the delights of the chocolate they

Air Raids

The local cricket field [Droylsden] nearby was taken over by the RAF with barrage balloons and searchlights. This was adventure for the local children, who loved talking to these men in uniform with strange accents, unlike our own. We asked where they lived before the war but the places were unknown to us in our restricted environment. The enemy planes started to arrive. Air raid sirens sounded. From our bedroom window we saw the planes coming over low, their markings visible as the enemy. The local aircraft guns would thunder into life. The guns were mobile and we heard the whistle of shrapnel falling into the street. When all went quiet and the 'All Clear' sounded, we would dash into the street and collect the shrapnel, some still warm from the explosion of the shells. What treasure! We exchanged some of it for cigarette cards, marbles or whatever was on offer from other children. The larger shrapnel we kept, the envy of others.

Dorothy Lord

Took Your Gas Mask Everywhere

We had to go to school [Fairfield] in shifts, while they built the air raid shelters. You had to take with you everywhere your gas mask, a pair of overshoes because the ground would be wet, and a box of iron rations. The air raid shelters were in the grounds, in front of the school, where there's an open piece of ground.

Jeanne Margerison

Collecting the Shrapnel

There was situated off Lumb Lane between Willow Bank Farm and the corner of Daisy Nook, an Ack Ack gun battery and search lights, at what was then called the army camp. During the air raids by the Germans, it got a bit risky living around Littlemoss, for when the guns were shooting at the aircraft, we got a number of bombs dropped in retaliation. I remember Lumb Mill receiving a direct hit with an incendiary bomb and probably the nearest bomb to Jaum Farm,

where we lived, was one that landed adjacent to Crowhill Farm, which was next to the white bridge. We, that night, were in the Anderson shelter, when that landed and we really felt the ground shake. After an air raid, next morning on my way to school, along Back and Plantation Lanes, I used to put the large lumps of shrapnel from the shells in the hedge, so as to collect them after school on my way home.

George Walker

I Missed the Air Raid

I got my baby, Peter, and then the war started. I used to get up and I had a table in that corner and I used to go under the table. My mother owned an air raid shelter at No. 12, Saxon Drive and John wouldn't get up and Irene wouldn't get up – no matter what you said. I think they dropped a bomb at the back here of the Delta and it was all lit up. I used to run down to my mother's with Peter and go in the shelter. Sometimes I would waken up and, when I got to the shelter, no-one was in it but I used to go in it. I used to think 'I wonder why they haven't got up?' because my mother and father were usually in first. It was the 'All Clear': I'd missed the first one!

Florence Dyson

Get Under Your Beds

When I was having Eileen, my husband used to say, 'Come on, get up!' But somehow I wasn't afraid. 'If another comes over, I'll get up'. The day Eileen was born, just a couple of hours after, in the Lake Hospital (part of Ashton Hospital now), there was a day air

A school photograph taken in May 1949 at Fairfield High School for Girls, Droylsden. On the left in the background are the air raid shelters used by the pupils. Margaret Walker is seated third row from the front, second left.

raid. They took me into the ward and all the babies had to go down in the shelter. So somebody said, 'What about the mothers?' Matron said, 'If it gets too bad, all get under your beds!' When it was nights and the bombs, there used to be a lot of shrapnel falling, which was dangerous. I lived in this street and my sister lived at the top. When the sirens went and I was on my own, her husband used to come down for me to go and sit in their shelter. I used to have my husband's tin hat on and I used to take the back off the cooker and put all this over Eileen, our baby's head, to stop the shrapnel falling and we used to walk up the back. You could tell a German plane and you could tell an English plane. A German plane went 'Rrh rrh'. An English was

all constant. The council then built shelters or they gave you shelters. You had an indoor one – a table one, a Morrison shelter, and my mother had an Anderson outside. Then they built one in a passage. We took deck chairs and sat in there, until they said, 'The roof's not suitable: don't go in there any more!'

Vera Worth

Dropping Bombs

A bomb dropped on Audenshaw cemetery and it smashed or cracked nearly all the people's windows, right up to Guide Bridge. Once they found the reservoirs, the pilots

98

knew roughly where the Northern Aircraft were up on the one side and the rubber works was supposedly a target as well. Northern Aircraft at Guide Bridge in South Street, Audenshaw, built aircraft parts.

Harry Slater

The Manchester Blitz

I remember the night of the Manchester Blitz. We were visiting some friends of Mum and Dad up Thornhill Road, which is up Moorside, and we could hear the bombs and see the light of the fires burning in Manchester. We were just stood outside watching. All the sky was lit up, terrible really, but of course for a young person it's excitement: it's something a little bit different. After the Blitz, we went down as far as we could in the lorry to Manchester. My father, myself and my uncle Fred, dropped the lorry and then we walked into Manchester. I remember standing on the corner where Woolworth's was, looking across Piccadilly and seeing everything completely flattened. I remember crunching through everywhere: every street was filled with glass. We stood on the corner and looked. Piccadilly was just unrecognisable, just the odd doorway standing and policemen there stopping

Florence Dyson, aged about seventeen, before her marriage to John Dyson (on the right), in the early 1930s. As an employee at Delta Works, John was taken annually by his employer Austin Hopkinson to Belgium, where here he is standing in a First World War trench.

The main entrance to Planet Foundry on Corporation Road, Audenshaw. Over the doorway is the date 1900. On the right the first door leads to the offices and the second is for the workers to clock in through and on the left is the pattern shop with the foundry further left.

people from taking things out of shop windows – absolutely devastated and still smoke and fire.

Fred Lord

War Work

My husband was still at Pikrose during the war. I remember him going out at night and being on Home Guard and going round the waterworks, because the pilots could see the water. They knew where they were when they saw the waterworks. He didn't go [into the Forces], because he was an engineer. So he was reserved but

my sister, Anne, they sent her. You couldn't go where you wanted if you were in a job that wasn't for the war. She finished up at the Delta and she couldn't file. She worked with John. At the end of the day, to make it look as though she'd been working, they used to do a little bit for her.

Florence Dyson

Doing the Men's Jobs

My mother worked for Arnfield's on Guide Lane and my father worked at Metrovic's at Openshaw. She was on a small lathe, which was, of course, man's work. She actually lost a finger while working on it. They were quite long hours, both for my mother and father. He was a 'chaser'. He had to make sure that things kept moving in the office.

Bill Pollitt

Worked to Drawings

At General Gas we made quick release boxes for pilots. We also made landing craft for use in the invasion of Europe later on. It was quite remarkable, because no one knew much about boats and we just had to work to drawings. The first one that we made in Planet Foundry, it was far too big to get out of the doors and they had to knock out a big section at the front of the factory. It was quite a great occasion: it was put on a huge low-loader lorry and the managing director's wife launched this onto Planet Foundry road. It was called a 'LCM7' – Landing Craft

Man; '7' must have been just the number of the design. There was a great cheer as this low loader started chugging out of Corporation Road and went to the Manchester Ship Canal somewhere. We were all very interested as to how it had fared. We received no word at all from the Admiralty. So after about a month, the managing director sent the Inspector of Naval Ordnance a letter to say, 'Has it passed all its tests?' He got a telegram back to say, 'Many killed by flying rivet heads!' Just a huge joke! So we presumed it was alright. We made several more after that.

David Langridge

Under the Table

We used to like it when the air raids went on, because, if the 'All Clear' hadn't gone by ten o'clock in the evening, we didn't have to go to school until ten o'clock the following morning. My grandfather was an Air Raid Warden. He used to have to put his tin hat on, take his stirrup pump and off he'd go. He just used to stride off and left grandma and I alone on this great big farm. They had aircraft guns in Guide Bridge station yard and they came across once and bombed, aiming, we thought, for the Northern Aircraft, which was just over Guide Bridge. The blast of a bomb coming down there knocked the grandfather clock over in my grandma's front room. Well, we thought we'd been hit. The pair of us were under the table, just the two of us together. My grandma was only about 'this big'! We laughed afterwards.

Betty Slater

ARP Warden

Our pantry was only about a yard wide and about two yards long under the staircase. I made a little wooden platform and we put a mattress on it and my mother and I used to sleep in there most nights for months and months, because we thought, 'If the sirens go, we'll have to come down'. I was in charge as my father was on duty. He was the ARP warden chief; he was based at a house, which was the main office about three or four doors away from Red Hall church. He used to take the phone calls there. They used to say, 'The planes are coming over: they've arrived in Manchester and they'll be

Betty Slater (née Gregory) on an outing and wearing her Fairfield High School blazer, in the 1940s.

coming over about half past ten, so be prepared'. He used to go out and do demonstrations at factories and schools, showing them how to deal with incendiary bombs, if they dropped. You couldn't put water directly on them, else it used to fly all over the place. He also gave lectures to other ARP wardens in the area, as they were installed. I was in the Air Training Corps and they used to take us to use the cellars of Northern Aircraft from the grammar school on Stamford Road, one or two nights a month, for rifle and target practice. The cellar had all been sandbagged. We had our targets way off in the distance and we used to lie down and do the firing down there.

Harry Slater

The Fireman Got In

I used to come home, have my tea, get ready and go to Trafalgar House, which used to be the orphanage. I used to be on until six in the morning, answering the phone and back to work next morning, but we were allowed to go to bed – we were on call. We had to put our own beds up every night; there were so many of us girls on a watch. One of them was a really comical girl. She got up one morning. She said, 'Oh, my back does hurt! These beds are horrible.' Of course, when she had to make her bed up, one of the firemen had been in and put a tin hat into the bed! We used to lock the door, so they couldn't get in but it didn't make any difference, because

The Air Training Corps of Audenshaw Grammar School for boys on camp, in the early 1940s. First on the right in the front row sitting cross-legged is Harry Slater.

firemen they just put this ladder up at the window.

Margaret Slater

We Want our Chips!

We had our own defence point [at General Gas Appliances]. I used to go on fire watching duty. We wanted to have some chips and the Home Guard Corporal wouldn't let us go out at all. We knew that there was one office on a mezzanine floor in the workshop and, if we climbed up that, we could climb through a window and get out through the roof. The Home Guard must have come into the Fire Guard room, whilst we were out, and realised that we'd gone out for the chips. We came back into the factory by the same route into the press shop. Of course all the lights were out in the factory but we knew our way. We made a noise and we suddenly heard someone shout, 'They've come over there' and all these men were running after us. We were dodging from place to place. They all had torches. We had nothing, except the chips. That should have been a good guide but eventually they trapped us into one room, where there was a big machine in one corner, called a sand blast machine. It was a big, cylindrical thing with a door in and we climbed into this and closed the door. These two lots of Home Guards came in into this room and they thought they'd trapped us. When they met one another they just couldn't understand where we'd gone. We got back quite safely without them finding us!

David Langridge

A Near Miss!

As a junior draughtsman [at General Gas], the first job every morning was to take a rifle and ten rounds of ammunition from the Home Guard lock-up store, where the commissioner off the gates had to unlock all this for me. I took them into the Chief Draughtsman's office, because he was the Lieutenant in charge of the Home Guard Unit. He was prepared if Germans suddenly dropped in front of General Gas Appliances; he was there with his gun and ten rounds of ammunition. The last job at night was taking them back and putting them away.

After I'd been doing the job for about eight months, I became very important, because there was a junior brought in. The lad was twice as tall as me. He took this duty on. So I took him to pick the gun up and, whilst we were in this little guardroom, I thought I'd show what I'd learned whilst I was doing this job. So I got the ten rounds of ammunition, and they were in clips, which each held five rounds of ammunition. So I showed him how you could insert the clip, push the bullets and push them down into the magazine, how you could push the bolt forward and the one round of ammunition would go into position for firing and, if you pulled the trigger, it fired. If you weren't going to pull the trigger, then you pulled the bolt back and that pulled the round of ammunition out. I pulled backwards and the round of ammunition didn't come out. When I tried to push it forwards again, there was another bullet trying to force its way in. The gun was faulty. We were in a little bit of a panic but I managed to prize all these remaining bullets out and then thought 'Thank goodness for that' and pushed the bolt home. I released the trigger, forgetting that there was already a bullet there that hadn't come out. I was kneeling on one knee with the gun pointing in the air and the lad was at the front of the gun. He thought, 'This is pointing at me,' and he put his head to one side. When I fired, it must have missed him by about three or four inches. It embedded itself in the roof. Nobody had heard this gun go off. We stood there transfixed for quite a few seconds. Then we had the presence of mind to put these four remaining bullets back in the clips, put them back in the ammunition store, take another five out, that were complete, and just walk into the drawing office, as if nothing had happened. Sometime later it would be found that one of the clips only had four bullets in it but we didn't own up. Nothing was ever said about this. They didn't notice the hole in the roof.

David Langridge

The Reality of War

One Saturday afternoon, we saw, passing slowly along one of the lines, a train filled with soldiers, many very dishevelled and a few bandaged, They had just been brought back from Dunkirk. As we cheered lustily from the fence, one of them threw us an orange, almost unobtainable at that time. It was one of the few occasions that we saw a little of the realities of the land war. There were regular appeals for money for the war and on our own initiative we made house to house collections for 'The Spitfire Fund', 'Salute the Soldier Fund' and 'The Aid to Russia Fund'. We only had two refusals, one from a man who thought we were lining our own pockets and one from a minister of religion who objected on political grounds

Members of the fire service on duty at Trafalgar House on Audenshaw Road during the war. Third from the left on the front row is Margaret Slater.

The cover of the work's pass allowing David Langridge to enter General Gas Appliances on Corporation Road, Audenshaw, issued in 1941.

to contributing to the Russians. We couldn't understand this, as we thought our enemy's enemy was our friend. We took great delight in taking the several pounds collected to the council offices at Ryecroft Hall, obtaining a receipt and looking for the details in the next edition of the local paper.

Arthur Bantoft

Testing the Explosion

The crates that carried these small $11\frac{1}{2}$ lb. bombs were sent to the RAF and then the crates came back empty [to General Gas]. On one occasion they came back with one of the bombs still in, and of course the works manager told the managing director, who said, 'I wonder what sort of explosion they get from these'. He went up to the back of the factory, climbed on the roof with the manager and they just lobbed it out. It landed and it made a much greater bang than they expected. It didn't do any real damage, except that there was a big oil drum out at the back of the factory, which had many shrapnel holes in it and it all just drained away. So nobody ever got in trouble over that, because it was the big man himself who had actually tried it out, the managing director. It was all hushed up but everybody in the factory knew!

David Langridge

Dorothy Clinton with her father, Bertram Worthington, outside her home at No. 107, Williamson Lane, Droylsden, in 1945, just after he had returned home from war service.

POWs

At Shepley were Italians on the land that was Audenshaw United football ground, which is on the new St Anne's Road. Quite a lot of the girls went talking to them. They used to make things; I had a cigarette box. They used to carve it out of any piece of wood and then they'd draw a picture on it and ink it in or paint it in.

Harry Slater

The Italians

I can see this picture of the Italian prisoners of war watching at the fence. There was a space where they could see through onto the showground [Audenshaw Gymkhana]. I can recall that they wore what looked like a denim type of jacket down to the waist, a very bright blue jacket with a bright red circle on the back, as I always thought was a target, so if they ever escaped there was something to aim for!

George Walker

Coming Home

Father went to India, whilst in the Forces. No more home leave. He wrote telling us of the poverty in the cities: beggars and disease and the heat. They went up into the mountains for their short leaves and they suffered prickly heat caused by the intense heat. When the war ended and the soldiers demobbed, they were issued with suits, shirts, overcoats and shoes. My father received his very coarse cloth, far from smart but warm and worn gratefully. I understand that some of the men had contracted scabies, whilst away on duty. This did spread to the civilians. Clothes had to be baked on removal in ovens to kill the mites; it was very contagious. Hot baths were necessary and then the skin coated with a white, sticky solution to kill the mites, which burrowed under the skin. It was another result of the war years.

Dorothy Lord

Dunkirk

I had a brother in the Grenadiers and he was at Dunkirk. He was only nineteen but he came through that alright. Then he joined the parachutes. Our worst time was when he was at Arnheim. When he came home, they dressed all the street up with flags.

Rose Perfect

Didn't Know My Dad

I was born on Williamson Lane in Droylsden, in February 1940, at the start of the war. My father had to go into the army in September 1940 so my mum was left with two very young children. I didn't see much of him because he was posted abroad, so I didn't really know him, only this soldier who I was shown photographs of. So when he came home and somebody

VE Day (Victory Europe) being celebrated in May 1945 in the back yard of Williamson Lane by Dorothy Clinton, her family and neighbours.

VE Day being celebrated in a street party on Easton Road, Droylsden, in 1945. Joyce Wild (eighth on the right) is sitting next to her brother, Ronald Goodwin and her mother is standing behind her.

told me my daddy was coming home, he was in civilian clothes and I just said, 'Are you my daddy?'

Dorothy Clinton

The Tin She Saved

In 1945 getting the food together must have been a problem, because of the rationing. My mum had a tin of tongue she had saved. Anyway my dad handed the tin of tongue in for the party. I bet he was in trouble with mum!

Joyce Wild

Street Parties

At the end of the war there was a big party in the street, a street party, VE day. Every child in the neighbourhood seemed to be there at these trestle tables and there was jelly and custard. There wasn't money for any extra clothing; you just had to use what you had. Mum would cut up things of hers to make kilts and dresses for me. Of course, clothing was still on coupons as well.

Dorothy Clinton

CHAPTER 7

Leisure

Members of Moorside Wesleyan chapel, Droylsden, taking part in the Whit Walks in the early 1900s.

Whit Walks

Our own Scholars' Walk really began on Whit Thursday evening, when my mother went out shopping for last minute touches, like white gloves, hair ribbons and flowers. Then there would be the 'trimming of the baskets', tall, thin shaped affairs with long handles that lent a certain splendour to a few irises, dog daisies and a bit of gypsy grass. Our procession started soon after nine [on Whit Friday] to the opening bars of 'Onward

Christian Soldiers', played by the Salvation Army Band. Slowly followed the big banner, borne high, proclaiming Red Hall Sunday school. After the banner came the little children, some only just able to toddle, and over them small, flower trimmed banners with such familiar texts as 'Feed my Lambs' and 'Suffer little children'.

After the children the older girls, self-conscious and a little shy in their new clothes and then came the boys, noisily shuffling, whistling, scuffling and cuffing one another. Close on their heels followed the mothers, content with, at best, a new hat, and the men, all stiff collars and bowlers and, here and there, a rose in the button hole. We would stop from time to time and sing from printed sheets, the grand old hymns of Charles Wesley. The way was long and the cobbles hard and uneven for feet in new shoes. Finally going through the gates of the farmyard adjoining our Sunday school, we were given a curranty bun and a blue striped mug of new farm milk. Later there would be sports and games, with prizes in the farmer's field, egg and spoon and skipping races, and more buns and milk.

Lena Slack

The 'String General'

I was a Sunday school teacher [at Bridge Street]. I walked with the infants. They used to have long strings for the children to get hold of. I used to be the 'string general'! They always had new, white clothes for Whit Walks and walked under the banner. Afterwards they generally had a farm field to play in.

Ruth Rogerson

Hand-me-downs!

It always had to be new clothes for Whit Sunday. I always remember with my sisters,

The Whit Walk procession passing the Primitive Methodist chapel on Moorside Lane, Droylsden, around 1931. On the right at the front is Jeanne Margerison (née Nixon).

we were all dressed alike and then the next year, they'd be handed down as there were three of us. Our Brenda, the last, was absolutely sick of those clothes; she got them three years on the run. We always had a basket of flowers and Gorton Silver Band played for years and years and years.

Betty Slater

New Clothes

We either had a *new* cap or a *new* blazer or a *new* pair of trousers or a striped tie with the stripe going horizontally, a great big knotted tie under your chin. If you were very, very lucky, then you got a cap *and* a blazer *and* a tie *and* sometimes you got new socks as well. The thrill of it for the boys, when we went to the Sunday school after the whit walk, you had a bottle of milk and a raspberry bun: it was like a rock cake with a raspberry blob in the middle. You stuck your finger in it. Then you used to go round to your uncles and aunties and grandmas and granddads in your blazer with your pocket open at the side and say, 'Do you like my new blazer and my new cap?' They used to put 3d bits in your pocket and if you were very, very lucky, you got a 6d piece. Then you used to go home and your mum and dad used to say, 'How much have you got?' You used to pour the money out onto the table and count it. It was a big day of the year. My clothes always came from the Arcadia in Ashton. My mother used to be in a club there and she used to pay all during the year and then we used to go and ask how much was in it and that used to decide whether it was a cap or trousers or both.

Harry Slater

Holy City

We used to walk all round the 'Holy City' – Hazel Street, Hawthorn Street, Corporation Road. I remember those big blank walls where the men used to lean the banners up, because they were heavy. All those big men that had to carry the banner from St Hilda's, while we stopped and sang hymns they don't sing nowadays. They used to sing 'Beautiful Zion built above, beautiful city that I love'.

Bessie Watt

A Long Day

We used to go very early to the cemetery, collect leaves and flowers and make them all crooks: they let us go in the conservatory, for the children to carry them to walk at Whit Friday. We used to come out of Bridge Street, go up Dale Street and along West Street, come back down Lord Street, then we used to go over the bridge and went as far as Birch Street, because a lot of people came from Birch Street to Bridge Street. Then we'd come back round Audenshaw Road: it used to be a long walk and down Stamford Road back to Bridge Street. We used to have a field day then, games on the cricket pitch on Woodbridge Avenue, before they built there. It was all fields.

Rose Perfect

'Will I Do?'

There was a little bit of rivalry between the churches. The Methodists' was on Shepley Road and there was St Hilda's, Bridge Street and Guide Lane. They used to sell little

A Whit Walk procession in Hooley Hill along Denton Road, Audenshaw, in the early 1900s. In the distance is the chimney of a factory on Pitt Street behind Charlie Smith's shop.

walking sticks for boys, imitation Charlie Chaplin, and they were $\frac{1}{2}$d each. Of course every lad had them and they were bashing each other as they passed. 'Who's hit me?' 'It weren't me!' When you was walking, you had a rope and the teacher was leading, pulling this rope and the children were holding on to it. There were flowers every so far fastened to this rope. Where we lived in Water Street, it was level with Guide Lane and there were no houses: there was a croft in between.

Vera Worth

Sunday School

I went to St Stephen's Sunday school. I had this lovely basket with a long handle and fluted round and, with my mother and father being in the market garden business and my mother stood Manchester markets at Smithfield, she always made me up, or had made a lovely basket. We went to the Sunday school for the bun and milk; it was more like a big muffin with a bit of sugar on.

Alice Adams

Droylsden's Gala Queen

Early in 1949, a number of us used to attend the dances at the Co-op Hall in Market Street. One particular night, the Gala committee had organized a function to choose a Gala Queen and her attendants. So in an absolute fit of bravado, because I was really very shy, I entered this Gala Queen procession, which took place in the hall itself. Eight young ladies finally paraded

112

round; to my utter amazement, I was selected and the remaining young ladies acted as Ladies-in-waiting for the crowning ceremony. I later found out that I was the third Droylsden Gala Queen to be elected for the Droylsden Sports Gala and Show, held at the Moorside Stadium. Not only did myself and all the ladies appear but there was Droylsden Military Band, teas, light refreshments, ice cream, donkey rides and a round-about. The attraction really was the Horse, Rabbit, Horticultural and Poultry Shows and Sheepdog Trial exhibitions and I was mentioned at the end of all that as the Gala Queen! The dress that I wore on the day was in white. I had, what we used to call, sweetheart necks and there was a brooch at each side, with a full bodice, long sleeves, a fitted waist and not a full skirt. It

was what I would call semi-straight. I had a bouquet of cream tea roses and pink carnations with greenery trailing down. It was all rather grand, I thought. I was presented with a compact by the committee and inscribed on the front was 'Droylsden Gala Queen 1949'.

During the year of office, we attended many functions that various churches held. I had no knowledge at all of football and I wasn't even remotely interested but I was asked to go to Droylsden cricket ground and kick off for the start of the [football] match. I was petrified over this and when I went on the field and kicked the ball, somebody said to me 'You've kicked it in the wrong direction!'

Dorothy Lord

Members of St Andrew's church on their Whit Walk, passing over Edge Lane canal bridge, Droylsden, in 1953. Joyce Wild's brother, David Goodwin, is the cushion bearer, second right from the front, and on the right in the background is St Andrew's church.

Audenshaw Carnival

One of the highlights of the year was the carnival, held in June to raise money for the local hospital. In 1926, my sister and I entered the 'Fancy Dress Children' section. My mother made my sister a crinoline and the loveliest poke bonnet and then borrowed lace mittens and a real Paisley shawl to complete the outfit. I was to be 'Bo-Peep', because my mother had recently made the costume for a cousin of mine. We assembled on the local football ground and lined up for the judging. I was only six years' old and had already walked two miles to the assembly point. Someone gave me a card to carry, with the magic words, 'Second Prize' and my delight was unbounded when I found my sister carrying a card which said, 'First Prize'. We were given sealed envelopes: my sister's contained 5s and mine 2s 6d and my mother was so pleased, you'd have thought we'd won a fortune.

Lena Slack

Carnival King

In the 1930s, my father used to dress up the horse that he used on the fish round and put ribbons and feathers on it. One year we hired a little black and white dappled pony and I rode that. I was dressed as an Indian with all the make-up and my father walked at my side. It used to go along Guide Lane up Stamford Road and finish at Ryecroft Hall. My father eventually became the 'Carnival King' with an uncle [not by

Dorothy Lord (née Vardy), as Droylsden's Gala Queen, together with her retinue, at the Droylsden Show in July 1949. The show was held in the Moorside Stadium.

Winners of the children's section of the fancy dress at Audenshaw Carnival in 1926. On the right stands Lena Slack aged six and on the left is her elder sister Elizabeth (Betty) Johnson.

birth], Albert Green, who was 'Carnival Queen'. For a few years we had this king and queen. I was a cushion bearer at one time.

Harry Slater

May Queen in Droylsden

I was an attendant to the May Queen one year. I think, really, the criteria for being an attendant or a queen was who'd got a long, white dress. I remember the head teacher saying, 'Put up your hand, if you'd got a long, white dress.' That was it. You were picked. I was about eight or nine

probably. We paraded around and all the mothers came to watch.

Jeanne Margerison

Decorating the Horses

There was a very old tradition, when the horse drawn vehicles were used, that on the 1st May, they were all decorated by using raffia and raffia type straw and ribbons and some people used bells as well, decorating the manes of the horses and also the tails.

George Walker

Joan Salthouse, the Rose Queen of Bridge Street Congregational church, Audenshaw, at Ryecroft Hall, in 1935. On the left is Jean Gregory and at the front cushion bearer Harry Slater. Jean is Betty Slater's sister and Harry is Betty's husband.

Jeanne Margerison (née Nixon), on the right aged about nine, as attendant with Marjorie Lee to the May Queen Margaret Boardman at Moorside School, Droylsden, in the mid-1930s.

Rose Queen

In the 1920s at Sunday school we were asked if we wanted to be attendants. They chose the rose queen. We were crowned in the Sunday school I think and then we came across to have photos taken with Mrs Hibbert in her garden. The Hibberts were an old Audenshaw family on Denton Road, overlooking the grammar school playing fields.

Joan Jebb

Margaret Slater's daughter Kathryn as Rose Queen of St Stephen's church, Audenshaw, in 1955. Here she takes part in the Whit Walks on Audenshaw Road near Groby Road.

Audenshaw Gymkhana

My elder brother Jack became the ringmaster of the annual Audenshaw Horse and

Gymkhana Show, which was held on a little football field, just off Denton Road, just a little further on from the Stamford cinema. It had a little wooden stand for people to sit in. Leonard Hartley, the grocer off Stockport Road, used to always show there. He was well known for his hackney type of horse, those with the high stepping front legs. Then there was a lady called Betty Malpas, a farmer's daughter from Denton. She was quite good at horse riding and always used to take part in the Audenshaw Horse and Gymkhana. The show probably finished just after the war [Second World War].

George Walker

Max Bygraves

We used to have the Gymkhana on this football ground and this particular year Max Bygraves came to open it. I wanted to do this particular number in one of the shows we were doing. I was dressed as a spiv and I had a Max Bygraves haircut at the time. So I wrote and asked and they sent me a letter to say 'Yes' I could do it. He was in a box area roped off for the Mayor and dignitaries. So I pushed my way through and said to him, 'I want to thank you for letting me do this.' We had a little chat.

Harry Slater

Crowning of the Rose Queen of St Hilda's church in Mrs Hibbert's garden on Denton Road, Audenshaw, around 1924. Mrs Hibbert stands in the middle at the back with the retiring queen on the left and the new queen, Carrie the vicarage maid, on the right. In the front row fourth from the left is Joan Jebb (née Thornley).

Audenshaw United football team (previously the YMCA team) at their ground off Denton Road, in the 1940s. On the right is David Langridge's father, Fred.

Moorside Trotting Stadium

There was a trotting track which was always there as long as I can remember. We used to play on there as well. There were two-wheeled sulkies: we'd pull one round and have rides on it.

Jeanne Margerison

Watching the Ponies

When I was at the primary school I can remember on the Moss there was Doddie's Trotting Stadium where they had these little carts behind the ponies. You could watch it from the road actually, you didn't have to go in to watch it.

John Pearson

The Tennis League

Lumb Lane tennis club was in the grounds of Lumb Lane Park up towards the railway. The teams were part of the Ashton tennis team. We had some wonderful players. We used to play in the league, certainly a couple of nights a week. Then we always had competitions on a Sunday and we had lots of happy hours there.

Margaret Walker

Tennis Courts

The ground, which is all turfed at the moment, used to have two hard courts on it, at the back. You see a raised up portion, which is like a terrace and that used to be flat and they had a hut on there. They used to run these tennis tournaments at the weekends and then they'd have an afternoon tea in the hut. It was the base for the old football team that they used to run, called Bridge Street football team. My father was running part of the team in the late 1920s to the 1940s, I think. They also had a cricket team that used the hut.

Harry Slater

Friendly Rivalry

When it came to leisure time [at Delta Works], there were cricket matches between Austin Hopkinson's own family, who were mostly public school people, and the workers.

Brenda Tunstall

Trafalgar Cricket Team

Where our house is built on Woodbridge Avenue is where the cricket pitch was in the early 1930s. Trafalgar Church had the cricket ground and they used to play every Saturday during the summer. They were in the Glossop League and every other Saturday they'd play at Charlesworth or Glossop or somewhere else. We used to travel with them. I was about fifteen or sixteen. We used to come into the pavilion

The Delta Works cricket team formed by Austin Hopkinson at an away match near London. They are at the home of Austin's brother, who is standing in the centre of the team, and whose family they played every Whitsuntide.

The YMCA on Denton Road, Audenshaw, where David Langridge lived as a boy, as his father was the caretaker. The family lived in the house on the right, which adjoined the YMCA.

and make tea for them at half-time. When Alan Dean bought this land to build these houses, they had to move then and they went to Boothcote, Mr Hammond's farm.

Margaret Slater

At the YMCA

My parents were the caretakers at the YMCA, No. 36, Denton Road, Audenshaw in the 1920s and 30s. On one occasion the young fellows from the football team were having a lark after a match and they carried one of the players out into the yard in the bath. He was absolutely naked, and he had to run back into the changing room. My mother happened to catch sight of him and these boys were brought in front of the committee and were made to come and apologize to my mother on the following Monday. We young boys from the family had to move out of the front room while these boys came in and made their apology.

There was also a wheelers' club for cyclists, who would always gather in front of the YMCA on Sunday mornings before setting out on their trips.

Mr Williams ran the library, a very gentle man. I think it was a ha'penny or a penny to borrow a book. My mother used to get books from the library. Of course, she didn't have to pay the ha'penny but she provided Mr Williams with cups of tea after he'd finished his stint.

David Langridge

Turned the Alarm Clock Off

I went to brownies at Fairfield. They met at the Moravian Sunday school. We wore these 'tea cosies', as they called it. I hated wearing them. We each had to go to Church Parade as well, of course, and, my brother and I didn't like it. We'd sneak into our mum and dad's bedroom and turn the alarm clock off, so we didn't actually have to go. I think dad realised, because I vaguely remember dad opening one eye and going back to sleep again. They knew what we were up to!

Kate Kerry

Prize Winner

Where Rose lived, they used to have like gardens, the men all round there. In September they used to have a horticultural show. There was an old man: he won the chrysants every time. My dad [Rose's] used to win with the potatoes. They sold them afterwards: you could buy them. They used to have a band at night. When the show was on, they'd great big gates they used to throw wide open from Dale Street. It was the highlight of the year.

Rose Perfect and Vera Worth

St Mary's Scouts

St Mary's scouts had then a wooden hut on Allen Street and it was given by a man called John Dean who worked for Robertson's. He bought the land and gave the land to the church for the scouts. Really

The cast of the Gangshow of St Mary's Droylsden Scouts in 1946. On the front row fourth from the right is John Pearson.

Fred Clark's father Walter in his garden in July 1928. Walter worked at Scott & Hodson's foundry but found time to tend his garden, including a large greenhouse and an allotment, plus keep poultry at his homes, first at Nelson Street and then at Denton Road.

that was my biggest amusement, from ten till seventeen, the scouts at Allen Street and going camping.

John Pearson

On the Allotments

In the 1930s, there used to be allotments behind the cemetery in Drolysden and I used to have to go there on a Sunday to a Mr Clayton who sold chrysanthemums. He used to tell me all about his plants and how he looked after them. I was very young. My dad had an allotment at the other end to Mr Clayton's, near the fairysteps.

Joyce Wild

Digging For Victory

My dad had an allotment down the bottom of Shepley Road by the river Tame. The river went round and it was very fertile ground. Of course, during the First World War, 'you dug for victory', didn't you. He must have grown enough potatoes to keep us in potatoes all year and cabbage, onions and carrots. I think dad was a very hard working man, because he not only worked hard in the foundry but then he had this place next to our house in Nelson Street, where we kept hens, and he had this big allotment down there. I can remember him wheeling me in the wheelbarrow down Shepley Road to this allotment.

We kept hens; we must have had at least forty or fifty. We had white Leghorns, and Rhode Island Reds. About Easter time, dad used to buy day-old chicks that came by train in a big container. We used to have them in the house, in the fireplace in this box, because they had to be warm. Sometimes they died unfortunately; sometimes they were dead when they arrived.

We had a big greenhouse. It had a brick base. It had pipes going through it. We had a little boiler house, you know. I think dad was jealous of Uncle Jim, because he grew orchids; he had three big greenhouses full of orchids.

Fred Clark

On Stage

They put shows on at our church [Bridge Street] and they also had a good society at Shepley Road. Then the pantomimes came and then reviews, a list of songs we'd like to sing and then someone would write words as a link to go through it. They were very successful. After that it went to the plays, mostly comedies: we just ran for the whole week. When we had the pantomimes, we used to run for the fortnight. We could fill that church, people sitting on window sills. They went down very, very well. Comedy was my forté [Harry]; I never played Buttons. I was the Dame or the mother in 'Cinderella'. The first pantomime we did was 'Babes in the Wood' and I was one of the broker's men.

Betty and Harry Slater

Harry and Betty Slater dressed up to appear in a review at Bridge Street Congregational church in the 1940s.

Noblett's Annual Trip

The whole workforce was taken on a day's outing. One of the first my mother Annie remembered, in the early 1900s, was a visit to the Lake District by train to Windermere, boat to Waterhead and then by horse drawn wagonette to Grasmere over Red Bank, where they walked up the steep slope to save the horses. It was a trip into a new world.

Arthur Bantoft

Noblett's Shilling

The coaches used to pull up outside Noblett's. One time he gave them a shilling and they called it Noblett's shilling. My dad still had his up to his dying day: it was for tea when he went on these trips and he never spent it!

Dorothy Clinton

At the Pub

The Blue Pig, in the early 1900s, was a much smaller building with a low roof, which was later raised. The landlord was Mr Yates and it was a well-run, respectable establishment. On the site of the car park was a bowling green, where granddad showed his skill. Between this and the back of the pub there were tables and benches. By the seats were a few cages where animals were kept: my mother remembered a badger and a monkey. The clientele included local people and 'the

123

passing trade', wagonette parties on the way to Belle Vue from Ashton. Music was restricted to a paid pianist on a Saturday night. One feature was the provision of hot coffee at six in the morning for people going to work.

Arthur Bantoft

Couldn't Get Rid of It!

A tale my dad told me once: there were some dud coins about, like a 2s piece or a 1s, which was a lot of money in those days. He said this money was spent in the Church Inn and they realised it was dud money. So they gave it to this person and said, 'Take a jug and go across to this pub and get a pint of tupenny'. So whoever it was went across and got this pint and didn't say it was for the Church Inn, to get rid of this dud coin. Whoever did the errand, they got the beer and they gave the change then back to the Church Inn. About an hour later someone else came in and they got this dud coin back!

Alice Adams

Making Music

The barrel organs and street singers came round and brought a bit more music into life, although to hear an old man or woman walk our street singing for pennies was dreadful but we always managed to find them a drink of tea.

My father had a melodeon, a sort of oblong version of the concertina, and he often sat down on a home-made wooden buffet and played chiefly hymns. When we acquired a

The Band of Hope at Bridge Street Congregational church, Audenshaw, in the early 1900s. Third from the right at the front is Ruth Rogerson (née Hall), who, born in 1898, at the age of one hundred and two recorded memories of her life.

Crowning of Harry Slater as Audenshaw's Carnival king and Albert Green as his queen, in the foyer of the Odeon cinema at Guide Bridge, in the 1950s. First on the right is the cinema manager, then Fred Cowperthwaite next to the Chairman of the council Ephraim Hewitt. On the left is house builder Alan Dean with his daughter Norma.

cabinet gramophone, my father had many favourites, played so often that I knew every note to the last fading note that led into the crackling noise, made as the needle ran off the final grooves at the edge of the record.

Lena Slack

The Band of Hope

I always went to the Band of Hope with Mr Jordan. They used to take us to Haughton Green and Denton Woods. Mr Jordan was a true Christian man. He worked at Jones' sewing machines and he used to be in his overalls. We had one lad and he was a boy soprano. He used to get this boy singing. 'Come on now: we'll have another hymn' and we did envy him. Really you didn't drink: you signed the pledge. 'Water, crystal water,' we used to sing. There was no other entertainment then. You had to go to church or you had to sit in your house.

Vera Worth

Going to the Cinema

When we lived in Droylsden we went to the matinee at the Palace; it's quite derelict now but it's still there. We called it 'the bug hut'. You'd queue all the way round, right down Church Street, to go to the matinee to cowboys and Indians. It was always continued the next week, so you had to go to find out.

Dorothy Clinton

Palace Cinema

We used to go with my mum and dad. In those days the queue from the Palace cinema used to stretch round the corner and right down Henry Street. Of course you could queue up there for an hour and not get in at the end of that hour, be turned away. There were shows like 'Old Mother Reilly' and 'George Formby'. I think the first six or eight rows were upholstered, wooden seats. For those you didn't go in at the front entrance but in at the back of the cinema. There was a little pay box there where you paid your money and you went and sat right by the screen. For all the other seats and the balcony you went through the front door. We used to collect jam jars and papers. The children used to go on a Saturday morn and they'd have big bags and containers there where you could put this stuff in, ready for the Saturday afternoon matinee. People collected aluminium pans, for the war effort. Nearly all jam jars were returnable and beer and milk bottles and usually you got a penny for how many you took. Sometimes Saturday morning running round with those and dropping them off, paid for your entrance to the cinema. At Christmas there used to be a free show for the children and when you went in, everybody got an orange and an apple. That was quite a treat at Christmas. You were lucky if you could get in.

Fred Lord

Odeon

I remember going, I think, every night of the week to see 'Love Letters' at the Odeon at Guide Bridge. We used to go there quite regularly – 2s 3d upstairs and 1s 9d downstairs.

Betty Slater

Local Cinemas

We went to Guide Bridge: where St Paul's is now was the Odeon and we used to go there as teenagers and see Doris Day. I loved her films and you would come back along Audenshaw Road singing the Doris Day songs. I can remember going to the Stamford on my thirteenth birthday. My mum wasn't very well and my dad took me to see the Great Caruso. That was a nice little cinema, a homely cinema.

Dorothy Clinton

Chips on the Way Home

We used to go to the Odeon, on a Saturday morning. There was the 6d club, the Mickey Mouse club, and the man that was the manager there looked like Mickey Mouse. He was about the same size and he had glasses on. There was a serial that was on there every week: it was 'Flash Gordon and the Clay Men' or 'Flash Gordon and the … ' etc. It ended just at that point when he was going to get killed and you had to go next week and pay your 6d. You had a club card and so it was quite important.

I used to go to the Stamford with my mother and father. My mother used to say,

Left: the cover of the monthly programme card of the Odeon cinema at Guide Bridge in 1955. Right: an advertisement of 1949 for the Stamford cinema, after it had been revamped and improved to become the 'New Stamford' on Stamford Road at the corner of Denton Road, Audenshaw.

'Now, we're going to the Stamford to the cinema but you've got to promise that you'll walk home!' Invariably, when we came out of the cinema, I was always dead tired and I had to be carried on my dad's shoulders and my mother used to play Hamlet with me! One of the treats on the way home, we used to stop at a chip shop, which is where Nigel Watson's car showroom is, and we used to get a penny worth of chips. I think it was ½d for peas. If I'd been *very* good, we might have a fish between the three of us. At the Stamford invariably the film used to break down halfway through and there'd be cheers and shouting.

Harry Slater

The Stamford

In the late '40s the Stamford became very, very important. It was all flat and then they put a sort of balcony, a raised section of about six rows, and you had to pay to go upstairs in the 'New Stamford'. Before, it also had just a walk in off the pavement to the box office and, when they had the raise-up, they built three steps and had a little raised reception there and put another toilet in. Originally there was only one toilet right at the bottom, and you had to come all the way down. Everybody knew where you were going!

Harry and Betty Slater

Pea-shooters

We used to go every Saturday to the Stamford; you went in down the side on Stamford Road like the back door, and they had forms. They used to have the fellow that we used to call the 'chucker out' but he was the fire officer that used to be all splendid in uniform when he was at the front. Round the back he used to keep us lot in order, because some boys used to bring pea-shooters and do them at the screen. They had a stage with two pieces of masonry round. I think they had statues on them with lights on and round the back of one they had a piano. She played the music to represent what was happening: if horses were galloping she would play like Russ Conway's 'Side-Saddle'; if it was sad, soulful music she used to play. At the back, instead of having forms, they were tip-up seats, better than the ones further forward – they were more upholstered. Once there were far too many to sit on these seats in front, so a few, probably older boys he let sit on the first few seats at the back. I was one that was pushed there and Edgar was with me and he shoved him on the forms. He started crying, 'He's my brother' and finally he relented and let him come and sit with me because he was younger.

Fred Clark

Fred's Version

The Stamford was very nice; they had wooden seats at the front, that was the pennies. If you paid tuppence you sat on tip-up seats. People used to throw orange peel and all sorts of things around. We would all go to the pictures. We'd come home and I could see the tea all ready on the table and my father sat in his chair and my mum sat at a big fire. My father would say 'Well, did you enjoy it?' and Fred would pace up and down and tell everything that had happened, the whole picture, who shot who, from beginning to end!

Bessie Watt